English Men of Letters

EDITED BY JOHN MORLEY

BUNYAN

BUNYAN

BY

JAMES ANTHONY FROUDE

London

MACMILLAN AND CO.

1880

CONTENTS.

BUNYAN

BUNYAN.

CHAPTER I.

EARLY LIFE.

'I WAS of a low and inconsiderable generation, my father's house being of that rank that is meanest and most despised of all families in the land.' 'I never went to school, to Aristotle or Plato, but was brought up in my father's house in a very mean condition, among a company of poor countrymen.' 'Nevertheless, I bless God that by this door He brought me into the world to partake of the grace and life that is by Christ in His Gospel.' This is the account given of himself and his origin by a man whose writings have for two centuries affected the spiritual opinions of the English race in every part of the world more powerfully than any book or books, except the Bible.

John Bunyan was born at Elstow, a village near Bedford, in the year 1628. It was a memorable epoch in English history, for in that year the House of Commons extorted the consent of Charles I. to the Petition of Right. The stir of politics, however, did not reach the humble household into which the little boy was introduced. His father was hardly occupied in earning bread for his wife and children as a mender of pots and kettles : a tinker,

—working in neighbours' houses or at home, at such
business as might be brought to him. ' The Bunyans,'
says a friend, ' were of the national religion, as men of
that calling commonly were.'   Bunyan himself, in a passage which has been always understood to refer to his
father, describes him ' as an honest poor labouring man,
who, like Adam unparadised, had all the world to get his
bread in, and was very careful to maintain his family.'
In those days there were no village schools in England ;
the education of the poor was an apprenticeship to agri-
culture or handicraft ; their religion they learnt at home
or in church.   Young Bunyan was more fortunate.   In
Bedford there was a grammar school, which had been
founded in Queen Mary's time by the Lord Mayor of
London, Sir William Harper.   Hither, when he was old
enough to walk to and fro, over the mile of road between
Elstow and Bedford, the child was sent, if not to learn
Aristotle and Plato, to learn at least ' to read and write
according to the rate of other poor men's children.'

If religion was not taught at school, it was taught
with some care in the cottages and farmhouses by parents and masters.   It was common in many parts of
England, as late as the end of the last century, for the
farmers to gather their apprentices about them on Sunday
afternoons, and to teach them the Catechism.   Rude as was
Bunyan's home, religious notions of some kind had been
early and vividly impressed upon him.   He caught, indeed, the ordinary habits of the boys among whom he was
thrown.   He learnt to use bad language, and he often lied.
When a child's imagination is exceptionally active, the
temptations to untruth are correspondingly powerful.   The
inventive faculty has its dangers, and Bunyan was emi-
nently gifted in that way.   He was a violent, passionate

boy besides, and thus he says of himself that for lying and swearing he had no equal, and that his parents did not sufficiently correct him. Wickedness, he declares in his own remorseful story of his early years, became a second nature to him. But the estimate which a man forms of himself in later life, if he has arrived at any strong abhorrence of moral evil, is harsher than others at the time would have been likely to have formed. Even then the poor child's conscience must have been curiously sensitive, and it revenged itself upon him in singular tortures.

'My sins,' he says, 'did so offend the Lord that even in my childhood He did scare and affright me with fearful dreams, and did terrify me with dreadful visions. I have been in my bed greatly afflicted while asleep, with apprehensions of devils and wicked spirits, who still, as I then thought, laboured to draw me away with them, of which I could never be rid. I was afflicted with thoughts of the Day of Judgment night and day, trembling at the thoughts of the fearful torments of hell fire.' When, at ten years old, he was running about with his companions in 'his sports and childish vanities,' these terrors continually recurred to him, yet 'he would not let go his sins.'

Such a boy required rather to be encouraged than checked in seeking innocent amusements. Swearing and lying were definite faults which ought to have been corrected; but his parents, perhaps, saw that there was something unusual in the child. To them he probably appeared not worse than other boys, but considerably better. They may have thought it more likely that he would conquer his own bad inclinations by his own efforts, than that they could mend him by rough rebukes.

When he left school he would naturally have been

bound apprentice, but his father brought him up at his own trade. Thus he lived at home, and grew to manhood there, forming his ideas of men and things out of such opportunities as the Elstow neighbourhood afforded.

From the time when the Reformation brought them a translation of it, the Bible was the book most read—it was often the only book which was read—in humble English homes. Familiarity with the words had not yet trampled the sacred writings into practical barrenness. No doubts or questions had yet risen about the Bible's nature or origin. It was received as the authentic word of God Himself. The Old and New Testament alike represented the world as the scene of a struggle between good and evil spirits; and thus every ordinary incident of daily life was an instance or illustration of God's Providence. This was the universal popular belief, not admitted only by the intellect, but accepted and realised by the imagination. No one questioned it, save a few speculative philosophers in their closets. The statesman in the House of Commons, the judge on the Bench, the peasant in a midland village, interpreted literally by this rule the phenomena which they experienced or saw. They not only believed that God had miraculously governed the Israelites, but they believed that as directly and immediately He governed England in the seventeenth century. They not only believed that there had been a witch at Endor, but they believed that there were witches in their own villages, who had made compacts with the devil himself. They believed that the devil still literally walked the earth like a roaring lion: that he and the evil angels were perpetually labouring to destroy the souls of men; and that God was equally busy overthrowing the devil's work, and bringing sin and crimes to eventual punishment.

In this light the common events of life were actually looked at and understood, and the air was filled with anecdotes so told as to illustrate the belief. These stories and these experiences were Bunyan's early mental food. One of them, which had deeply impressed the imagination of the Midland counties, was the story of 'Old Tod.' This man came one day into court, in the Summer Assizes at Bedford, 'all in a dung sweat,' to demand justice upon himself as a felon. No one had accused him, but God's judgment was not to be escaped, and he was forced to accuse himself. 'My Lord,' said Old Tod to the judge, 'I have been a thief from my childhood. I have been a thief ever since. There has not been a robbery committed these many years, within so many miles of this town, but I have been privy to it.' The judge, after a conference, agreed to indict him of certain felonies which he had acknowledged. He pleaded guilty, implicating his wife along with him, and they were both hanged.

An intense belief in the moral government of the world creates what it insists upon. Horror at sin forces the sinner to confess it, and makes others eager to punish it. 'God's revenge against murder and adultery' becomes thus an actual fact, and justifies the conviction in which it rises. Bunyan was specially attentive to accounts of judgments upon swearing, to which he was himself addicted. He tells a story of a man at Wimbledon, who, after uttering some strange blasphemy, was struck with sickness, and died cursing. Another such scene he probably witnessed himself,[1] and never forgot. An alehouse-keeper in the neighbourhood of Elstow had a son who was half-

[1] The story is told by Mr. Attentive in the 'Life of Mr. Badman;' but it is almost certain that Bunyan was relating his own experience.

witted. The favourite amusement, when a party was
collected drinking, was for the father to provoke the lad's
temper, and for the lad to curse his father and wish the
devil had him. The devil at last did have the alehouse-
keeper, and rent and tore him till he died. 'I,' says
Bunyan, 'was eye and ear witness of what I here say.
I have heard Ned in his roguery cursing his father, and
his father laughing thereat most heartily, still provoking
of Ned to curse that his mirth might be increased. I saw
his father also when he was possessed. I saw him in one
of his fits, and saw his flesh as it was thought gathered
up in an heap about the bigness of half an egg, to the
unutterable torture and affliction of the old man. There
was also one Freeman, who was more than an ordinary
doctor, sent for to cast out the devil, and I was there
when he attempted to do it. The manner whereof was
this. They had the possessed in an outroom, and laid
him upon his belly upon a form, with his head hanging
down over the form's end. Then they bound him down
thereto ; which done, they set a pan of coals under his
mouth, and put something therein which made a great
smoke—by this means, as it was said, to fetch out the devil.
There they kept the man till he was almost smothered in
the smoke, but no devil came out of him, at which Freeman was somewhat abashed, the man greatly afflicted,
and I made to go away wondering and fearing. In a
little time, therefore, that which possessed the man
carried him out of the world, according to the cursed
wishes of his son.'

The wretched alehouse-keeper's life was probably
sacrificed in this attempt to dispossess the devil. But the
incident would naturally leave its mark on the mind of
an impressionable boy. Bunyan ceased to frequent such

places after he began to lead a religious life. The story, therefore, most likely belongs to the experiences of his first youth after he left school ; and there may have been many more of a similar kind, for, except that he was steady at his trade, he grew up a wild lad, the ringleader of the village apprentices in all manner of mischief. He had no books, except a life of Sir Bevis of Southampton, which would not tend to sober him ; indeed, he soon forgot all that he had learnt at school, and took to amusements and doubtful adventures, orchard-robbing, perhaps, or poaching, since he hints that he might have brought himself within reach of the law. In the most passionate language of self-abhorrence, he accuses himself of all manner of sins, yet it is improbable that he appeared to others what in later life he appeared to himself. He judged his own conduct as he believed that it was regarded by his Maker, by whom he supposed eternal torment to have been assigned as the just retribution for the lightest offence. Yet he was never drunk. He who never forgot anything with which he could charge himself, would not have passed over drunkenness, if he could remember that he had been guilty of it ; and he distinctly asserts, also, that he was never in a single instance unchaste. In our days, a rough tinker who could say as much for himself after he had grown to manhood, would be regarded as a model of self-restraint. If, in Bedford and the neighbourhood, there was no young man more vicious than Bunyan, the moral standard of an English town in the seventeenth century must have been higher than believers in Progress will be pleased to allow.

He declares that he was without God in the world, and in the sense which he afterwards attached to the word this was probably true. But serious thoughts seldom

ceased to work in him. Dreams only reproduce the
forms and feelings with which the waking imagination is
most engaged. Bunyan's rest continued to be haunted
with the phantoms which had terrified him when a child.
He started in his sleep, and frightened the family with
his cries. He saw evil spirits in monstrous shapes and
fiends blowing flames out of their nostrils. 'Once,' says
a biographer, who knew him well, and had heard the
story of his visions from his own lips, ' he dreamed that
he saw the face of heaven as it were on fire, the firma-
ment crackling and shivering with the noise of mighty
thunder, and an archangel flew in the midst of heaven,
sounding a trumpet, and a glorious throne was seated in
the east, whereon sat One in brightness like the morning
star. Upon which, he thinking it was the end of the
world, fell upon his knees and said, " Oh, Lord, have
mercy on me ! What shall I do ? The Day of Judgment is come and I am not prepared." '

At another time ' he dreamed that he was in a pleasant place jovial and rioting, when an earthquake rent
the earth, out of which came bloody flames, and the
figures of men tossed up in globes of fire, and falling down
again with horrible cries and shrieks and execrations,
while devils mingled among them, and laughed aloud at
their torments. As he stood trembling, the earth sank
under him, and a circle of flames embraced him. But
when he fancied he was at the point to perish, One in
shining white raiment descended and plucked him out of
that dreadful place, while the devils cried after him to
take him to the punishment which his sins had deserved.
Yet he escaped the danger, and leapt for joy when he
awoke and found it was a dream.'

Mr. Southey, who thinks wisely that Bunyan's bio-

graphers have exaggerated his early faults, considers that
at worst he was a sort of ʻ blackguard.' This, too, is a
wrong word. Young village blackguards do not dream
of archangels flying through the midst of heaven, nor
were these imaginations invented afterwards, or rhetori-
cally exaggerated. Bunyan was undoubtedly given to
story-telling as a boy, and the recollection of it made
him peculiarly scrupulous in his statements in later life.
One trait he mentions of himself which no one would
have thought of who had not experienced the feeling, yet
every person can understand it and sympathise with it.
These spectres and hobgoblins drove him wild. He says,
ʻ I was so overcome with despair of life and heaven, that
I should often wish either that there had been no hell, or
that I had been a devil ; supposing that they were only
tormentors, and that, if it must needs be that I went thither,
I might rather be a tormentor than tormented myself.'

The visions at last ceased. God left him to himself,
as he puts it, and gave him over to his own wicked inclinations. He fell, he says, into all kinds of vice and
ungodliness without further check. The expression is
very strong, yet when we look for particulars we can find
only that he was fond of games which Puritan preciseness
disapproved. He had high animal spirits, and engaged
in lawless enterprises. Once or twice he nearly lost his
life. He is sparing of details of his outward history,
for he regarded it as nothing but vanity ; but his escapes
from death were providences, and therefore he mentions
them. He must have gone to the coast somewhere, for
he was once almost drowned in a creek of the sea. He fell
out of a boat into the river at another time, and it seems
that he could not swim. Afterwards he seized hold of an
adder, and was not bitten by it. These mercies were sent

as warnings, but he says that he was too careless to profit
by them.   He thought that he had forgotten God altogether, and yet it is plain that he had not forgotten.   A
bad young man, who has shaken off religion because it is
a restraint, observes with malicious amusement the faults
of persons who make a profession of religion.   He infers
that they do not really believe it, and only differ from
their neighbours in being hypocrites.   Bunyan notes this
disposition in his own history of Mr. Badman.   Of himself, he says : ' Though I could sin with delight and ease,
and take pleasure in the villanies of my companions, even
then, if I saw wicked things done by them that professed
goodness, it would make my spirit tremble.   Once, when
I was in the height of my vanity, hearing one swear that
was reckoned a religious man, it made my heart to ache.'

He was now seventeen, and we can form a tolerably
accurate picture of him—a tall, active lad, working as
his father's apprentice, at his pots and kettles, ignorant
of books, and with no notion of the world beyond what
he could learn in his daily drudgery, and the talk of the
alehouse and the village green ; inventing lies to amuse
his companions, and swearing that they were true ;
playing bowls and tipcat, ready for any reckless action,
and always a leader in it, yet all the while singularly pure from the more brutal forms of vice, and
haunted with feverish thoughts, which he tried to forget
in amusements.   It has been the fashion to take his account of himself literally, and represent him as the worst
of reprobates, in order to magnify the effects of his conversion, and perhaps to make intelligible to his admiring
followers the reproaches which he heaps upon himself.
They may have felt that they could not be wrong in
explaining his own language in the only sense in which

they could attach a meaning to it. Yet, sinner though
he may have been, like all the rest of us, his sins were
not the sins of coarseness and vulgarity. They were the
sins of a youth of sensitive nature and very peculiar gifts :
gifts which brought special temptations with them, and
inclined him to be careless and desperate, yet from causes
singularly unlike those which are usually operative in
dissipated and uneducated boys.

It was now the year 1645. Naseby Field was near,
and the first Civil War was drawing to its close. At
this crisis Bunyan was, as he says, drawn to be a soldier ;
and it is extremely characteristic of him and of the body
to which he belonged, that he leaves us to guess on which
side he served. He does not tell us himself. His friends
in after life did not care to ask him, or he to inform them,
or else they also thought the matter of too small importance to be worth mentioning with exactness. There
were two traditions, and his biographers chose between
them as we do. Close as the connection was in that
great struggle between civil and religious liberty—flung
as Bunyan was flung into the very centre of the conflict
between the English people and the Crown and Church and
aristocracy—victim as he was himself of intolerance and
persecution, he never but once took any political part,
and then only in signing an address to Cromwell. He
never showed any active interest in political questions ;
and if he spoke on such questions at all after the Restoration, it was to advise submission to the Stuart Government. By the side of the stupendous issues of human
life, such miserable *rights* as men might pretend to in
this world were not worth contending for. The only
right of man that he thought much about, was the right to
be eternally damned if he did not lay hold of grace. King

and subject were alike creatures whose sole significance
lay in their individual immortal souls. Their relations
with one another upon earth were nothing in the presence
of the awful judgment which awaited them both. Thus
whether Bunyan's brief career in the army was under
Charles or under Fairfax must remain doubtful. Probability is on the side of his having been with the Royalists.
His father was of ' the national religion.' He himself
had as yet no special convictions of his own. John Gifford,
the Baptist minister at Bedford, had been a Royalist.
The only incident which Bunyan speaks of connected
with his military experience points in the same direction.
' When I was a soldier,' he says, ' I was with others
drawn out to go to such a place to besiege it. But when
I was just ready to go, one of the company desired to go
in my room. Coming to the siege as he stood sentinel
he was shot in the heart with a musket bullet and died.'
Tradition agrees that the place to which these words
refer was Leicester. Leicester was stormed by the King's
troops a few days before the battle of Naseby. It was
recovered afterwards by the Parliamentarians, but on the
second occasion there was no fighting, as it capitulated
without a shot being fired. Mr. Carlyle supposes that
Bunyan was not with the attacking party, but was in
the town as one of the garrison, and was taken prisoner
there. But this cannot be, for he says expressly that
he was one of the besiegers. Legend gathers freely about
eminent men, about men especially who are eminent in
religion, whether they are Catholic or Protestant. Lord
Macaulay is not only positive that the hero of the English
Dissenters fought on the side of the Commonwealth, but
he says, without a word of caution on the imperfection
of the evidence, ' His Greatheart, his Captain Boanerges,

and his Captain Credence, are evidently portraits of which
the originals were among those martial saints who fought
and expounded in Fairfax's army.' [1]

If the martial saints had impressed Bunyan so deeply,
it is inconceivable that he should have made no more al-
lusion to his military service than in this brief passage.
He refers to the siege and all connected with it merely as
another occasion of his own providential escapes from
death.

Let the truth of this be what it may, the troop to
which he belonged was soon disbanded. He returned at
the end of the year to his tinker's work at Elstow, much
as he had left it. The saints, if he had met with saints,
had not converted him. 'I sinned still,' he says, 'and
grew more and more rebellious against God and careless
of my own salvation.' An important change of another
kind, however, lay before him. Young as he was he
married. His friends advised it, for they thought that
marriage would make him steady. The step was less im-
prudent than it would have been had Bunyan been in a
higher rank of life, or had aimed at rising into it. The
girl whom he chose was a poor orphan, but she had been
carefully and piously brought up, and from her acceptance
of him, something more may be inferred about his character. Had he been a dissolute idle scamp, it is unlikely
that a respectable woman would have become his wife
when he was a mere boy. His sins, whatever these were,
had not injured his outward circumstances; it is clear
that all along he worked skilfully and industriously at
his tinkering business. He had none of the habits which
bring men to beggary. From the beginning of his life to

---

[1] *Life of Bunyan*: Collected Works, vol. vii. p. 299.

the end of it he was a prudent, careful man, and, considering
the station to which he belonged, a very successful man.

'I lighted on a wife,' he says, 'whose father was
counted godly. We came together as poor as poor might
be, not having so much household stuff as a dish or a
spoon between us. But she had for her portion two
books, "The Plain Man's Pathway to Heaven," and "The
Practice of Piety," which her father had left her when he
died. In these two books I sometimes read with her.
I found some things pleasing to me, but all this while I
met with no conviction. She often told me what a godly
man her father was, how he would reprove and correct
vice both in his house and among his neighbours, what
a strict and holy life he lived in his day both in word and
deed. These books, though they did not reach my heart,
did light in me some desire to religion.'

There was still an Established Church in England,
and the constitution of it had not yet been altered. The
Presbyterian platform threatened to take the place of
Episcopacy, and soon did take it ; but the clergyman was
still a priest and was still regarded with pious veneration
in the country districts as a semi-supernatural being.
The altar yet stood in its place, the minister still appeared
in his surplice, and the Prayers of the Liturgy continued
to be read or intoned. The old familiar bells, Catholic as
they were in all the emotions which they suggested, called
the congregation together with their musical peal, though
in the midst of triumphant Puritanism. The 'Book of
Sports,' which, under an order from Charles I., had been
read regularly in Church, had in 1644 been laid under a
ban ; but the gloom of a Presbyterian Sunday was, is,
and for ever will be detestable to the natural man ; and
the Elstow population gathered persistently after service

on the village green for their dancing, and their leaping, and their archery.   Long habit cannot be transformed in a day by an Edict of Council, and amidst army manifestoes and battles of Marston Moor, and a king dethroned and imprisoned, old English life in Bedfordshire preserved its familiar features.   These Sunday sports had been a special delight to Bunyan, and it is to them which he refers in the following passage, when speaking of his persistent wickedness.   On his marriage he became regular and respectable in his habits.   He says, 'I fell in with the religion of the times to go to church twice a day, very devoutly to say and sing as the others did, yet retaining my wicked life. Withal I was so overrun with the spirit of superstition that I adored with great devotion even all things, both the high place, priest, clerk, vestment, service, and what else belonging to the Church, counting all things holy therein contained, and especially the priest and clerk most happy and without doubt greatly blessed.   This conceit grew so strong in my spirit, that had I but seen a priest, though never so sordid and debauched in his life, I should find my spirit fall under him, reverence, and be knit to him.   Their name, their garb, and work did so intoxicate and bewitch me.'

Surely if there were no other evidence, these words would show that the writer of them had never listened to the expositions of the martial saints.

CHAPTER II.

CONVICTION OF SIN.

The 'Pilgrim's Progress' is the history of the struggle
of human nature to overcome temptation and shake off
the bondage of sin, under the convictions which prevailed
among serious men in England in the seventeenth century.
The allegory is the life of its author cast in an imaginative form. Every step in Christian's journey had been
first trodden by Bunyan himself; every pang of fear and
shame, every spasm of despair, every breath of hope and
consolation, which is there described, is but a reflexion as
on a mirror from personal experience. It has spoken to
the hearts of all later generations of Englishmen because
it came from the heart; because it is the true record of
the genuine emotions of a human soul; and to such a
record the emotions of other men will respond, as one
stringed instrument vibrates responsively to another.
The poet's power lies in creating sympathy; but he cannot,
however richly gifted, stir feelings which he has not himself known in all their intensity.

> Ut ridentibus arrident ita flentibus adflent
> Humani vultus.   Si vis me flere dolendum est
> Primum ipsi tibi.

The religious history of man is essentially the same in
all ages. It takes its rise in the duality of his nature. He

is an animal, and as an animal he desires bodily pleasure
and shrinks from bodily pain.   As a being capable of
morality, he is conscious that for him there exists a right
and wrong.   Something, whatever that something may
be, binds him to choose one and avoid the other.   This is
his religion, his religatio, his obligation, in the sense in
which the Romans, from whom we take it, used the word ;
and obligation implies some superior power to which man
owes obedience.   The conflict between his two dispositions
agitates his heart, and perplexes his intellect.   To do
what the superior power requires of him, he must thwart
his inclinations.   He dreads punishment, if he neglects to
do it.   He invents methods by which he can indulge his
appetites, and finds a substitute by which he can propitiate
his invisible ruler or rulers.   He offers sacrifices; he
institutes ceremonies and observances.   This is the religion of the body, the religion of fear.   It is what we
call superstition.   In his nobler moods he feels that this
is but to evade the difficulty.   He perceives that the sacrifice required is the sacrifice of himself.   It is not the
penalty for sin which he must fear, but the sin itself.   He
must conquer his own lower nature.   He must detach his
heart from his pleasures, and he must love good for its
own sake, and because it is his only real good ; and this is
spiritual religion or piety.   Between these two forms of
worship of the unseen, the human race has swayed to and
fro from the first moment in which they learnt to discern
between good and evil.   Superstition attracts, because it
is indulgent to immorality by providing means by which
God can be pacified.   But it carries its antidote along
with it, for it keeps alive the sense of God's existence ;
and when it has produced its natural effects, when the
believer rests in his observances and lives practically as if

there was no God at all, the conscience again awakes. Sacrifices and ceremonies become detested as idolatry, and religion becomes conviction of sin, a fiery determination to fight with the whole soul against appetite, vanity, self-seeking, and every mean propensity which the most sensitive alarm can detect. The battle unhappily is attended with many vicissitudes. The victory, though practically it may be won, is never wholly won. The struggle brings with it every variety of emotion, alternations of humility and confidence, despondency and hope. The essence of it is always the same—the effort of the higher nature to overcome the lower. The form of it varies from period to period, according to the conditions of the time, the temperament of different people, the conception of the character of the Supreme Power, which the state of knowledge enables men to form. It will be found even when the puzzled intellect can see no light in Heaven at all, in the stern and silent fulfilment of moral duty. It will appear as enthusiasm; it will appear as asceticism. It will appear wherever there is courage to sacrifice personal enjoyment for a cause believed to be holy. We must all live. We must all, as we suppose, in one shape or other give account for our actions; and accounts of the conflict are most individually interesting when it is an open wrestle with the enemy; as we find in the penances and austerities of the Catholic saints, or when the difficulties of belief are confessed and detailed, as in David's Psalms, or in the Epistles of St. Paul. St. Paul, like the rest of mankind, found a law in his members warring against the law which was in his heart. The problem presented to him was how one was to be brought into subjection to the other, and the solution was by 'the putting on of Christ.' St .Paul's mind was

charged with the ideas of Oriental and Greek philosophy
then prevalent in the Roman Empire. His hearers
understood him, because he spoke in the language of the
prevailing speculations. We who have not the clue cannot, perhaps, perfectly understand him; but his words
have been variously interpreted as human intelligence has
expanded, and have formed the basis of the two great
theologies which have been developed out of Christianity.
The Christian religion taught that evil could not be overcome by natural human strength. The Son of God had
come miraculously upon earth, had lived a life of stainless
purity, and had been offered as a sacrifice to redeem men
conditionally from the power of sin. The conditions, as
English Protestant theology understands them, are nowhere more completely represented than in the ' Pilgrim's
Progress.' The Catholic theology, rising as it did in the
two centuries immediately following St. Paul, approached
probably nearer to what he really intended to say.

Catholic theology, as a system, is a development of
Platonism. The Platonists had discovered that the seat
of moral evil was material substance. In matter, and
therefore in the human body, there was either some in-
herent imperfection, or some ingrained perversity and
antagonism to good. The soul so long as it was attached
to the body was necessarily infected by it; and as human
life on earth consisted in the connection of soul and body,
every single man was necessarily subject to infirmity.
Catholic theology accepted the position and formulated an
escape from it. The evil in matter was a fact. It was
explained by Adam's sin. But there it was. The taint
was inherited by all Adam's posterity. The flesh of man
was incurably vitiated, and if he was to be saved a new
body must be prepared for him. This Christ had done.

That Christ's body was not as other men's bodies was
proved after his resurrection, when it showed itself independent of the limitations of extended substance. In
virtue of these mysterious properties it became the body
of the Corporate Church into which believers were admitted by baptism. The natural body was not at once
destroyed, but a new element was introduced into it, by
the power of which, assisted by penance and mortifica-
tion, and the spiritual food of the Eucharist, the grosser
qualities were gradually subdued, and the corporeal
system was changed. Then body and spirit became alike
pure together, and the saint became capable of obedience,
so perfect as not only to suffice for himself, but to supply
the wants of others. The corruptible put on incorruption.
The bodies of the saints worked miracles, and their flesh
was found unaffected by decay after hundreds of years.

This belief so long as it was sincerely held issued
naturally in characters of extreme beauty; of beauty so
great as almost to demonstrate its truth. The purpose of
it, so far as it affected action, was self-conquest. Those
who try with their whole souls to conquer themselves
find the effort lightened by a conviction that they are receiving supernatural assistance; and the form in which
the Catholic theory supposed the assistance to be given
was at least perfectly innocent. But it is in the nature
of human speculations, though they may have been
entertained at first in entire good faith, to break down
under trial, if they are not in conformity with fact.
Catholic theology furnished Europe with a rule of faith
and action which lasted 1500 years. For the last three
centuries of that period it was changing from a religion
into a superstition, till, from being the world's guide, it
became its scandal. 'The body of Christ' had become a

kingdom of this world, insulting its subjects by the effron-
tery of its ministers, the insolence of its pretensions, the
mountains of lies which it was teaching as sacred truths.
Luther spoke ; and over half the Western world the
Catholic Church collapsed, and a new theory and Christianity had to be constructed out of the fragments of it.

There was left behind a fixed belief in God and in the
Bible as His revealed word, in a future judgment, in the
fall of man, in the atonement made for sin by the death
of Christ, and in the new life which was made possible
by His resurrection. The change was in the conception
of the method by which the atonement was imagined to
be efficacious. The material or sacramental view of it,
though it lingered inconsistently in the mind even of
Luther himself, was substantially gone. New ideas
adopted in enthusiasm are necessarily extreme. The
wrath of God was held to be inseparably and eternally
attached to every act of sin, however infirm the sinner.
That his nature could be changed, and that he could be
mystically strengthened by incorporation with Christ's
body in the Church was contrary to experience, and was
no longer credible. The conscience of every man, in the
Church or out of it, told him that he was daily and hourly
offending. God's law demanded a life of perfect obedience, eternal death being the penalty of the lightest breach
of it. No human being was capable of · such perfect
obedience. He could not do one single act which would
endure so strict a scrutiny. All mankind were thus included under sin. The Catholic Purgatory was swept
away. It had degenerated into a contrivance for feeding
the priests with money, and it implied that human nature
could in itself be renovated by its own sufferings. Thus
nothing lay before the whole race except everlasting

reprobation. But the door of hope had been opened on the cross of Christ. Christ had done what man could never do. He had fulfilled the law perfectly. God was ready to accept Christ's perfect righteousness as a substitute for the righteousness which man was required to present to him, but could not. The conditions of acceptance were no longer sacraments or outward acts, or lame and impotent efforts after a moral life, but faith in what Christ had done; a complete self-abnegation, a resigned consciousness of utter unworthiness, and an unreserved acceptance of the mercy held out through the Atonement. It might have been thought that since man was born so weak that it was impossible for him to do what the law required, consideration would be had for his imfirmity; that it was even dangerous to attribute to the Almighty a character so arbitrary as that He would exact an account from his creatures which the creature's necessary inadequacy rendered him incapable of meeting. But the impetuosity of the new theology would listen to no such excuses. God was infinitely pure, and nothing impure could stand in his sight. Man, so long as he rested on merit of his own, must be for ever excluded from his presence. He must accept grace on the terms on which it was held out to him. Then and then only God would extend his pity to him. He was no longer a child of wrath : he was God's child. His infirmities remained, but they were constantly obliterated by the merits of Christ. And he had strength given to him, partially, at least, to overcome temptation, under which, but for that strength, he would have fallen. Though nothing which he could do could deserve reward, yet he received grace in proportion to the firmness of his belief; and his efforts after obedience, imperfect though they might be, were accepted for Christ's sake. A good life, or a constant effort after a good life, was still the object which a man was bound to labour after. Though giving no claim to pardon, still less for reward, it was the necessary fruit of a sense of what Christ had done, and of love and gratitude towards him. Good works were the test of saving faith, and if there were no signs of them, the faith was barren : it was not real faith at all.

This was the Puritan belief in England in the seventeenth century. The reason starts at it, but all religion is paradoxical to reason. God hates sin, yet sin exists. He is omnipotent, yet evil is not overcome. The will of man is free, or there can be no guilt, yet the action of the will, so far as experience can throw light on its operation, is as much determined by antecedent causes as every other natural force. Prayer is addressed to a Being assumed to be omniscient, who knows better what is good for us than we can know, who sees our thoughts without requiring to hear them in words, whose will is fixed and cannot be changed. Prayer, therefore, in the eye of reason is an impertinence. The Puritan theology is not more open to objection on the ground of unreasonableness than the Catholic theology or any other which regards man as answerable to God for his conduct. We must judge of a creed by its effects on character, as we judge of the wholesomeness of food as it conduces to bodily health. And the creed which swept like a wave through England at that time, and recommended itself to the noblest and most powerful intellects, produced also in those who accepted it a horror of sin, an enthusiasm for justice, purity, and manliness, which can be paralleled only in the first age of Christianity. Certainly there never was such a theory to take man's conceit out of him. He was a

miserable wretch, so worthless at his best as to deserve
everlasting perdition. If he was to be saved at all, he
could be saved only by the unmerited grace of God. In
himself he was a child of the devil; and hell, not in
metaphor, but in hard and palpable fact, inevitably waited
for him. This belief, or the affectation of this belief,
continues to be professed, but without a realisation of its
tremendous meaning. The form of words is repeated by
multitudes who do not care to think what they are saying. Who can measure the effect of such a conviction
upon men who were in earnest about their souls, who
were assured that this account of their situation was
actually true, and on whom, therefore, it bore with in-
creasing weight in proportion to their sincerity?

With these few prefatory words, I now return to
Bunyan. He had begun to go regularly to church, and
by Church he meant the Church of England. The change
in the constitution of it, even when it came, did not much
alter its practical character in the country districts. At
Elstow, as we have seen, there was still a high place;
there was still a liturgy; there was still a surplice. The
Church of England is a compromise between the old
theology and the new. The Bishops have the apostolical
succession, but many of them disbelieve that they de-
rive any virtue from it. The clergyman is either a priest
who can absolve men from sins, or he is a minister as
in other Protestant communions. The sacraments are
either means of grace, or mere outward signs. A Christian is either saved by baptism, or saved by faith, as he
pleases to believe. In either case he may be a member of
the Church of England. The effect of such uncertain utter-
ances is to leave an impression that in defining such points
closely, theologians are laying down lines of doctrines

about subjects of which they know nothing, that the real truth of religion lies in what is common to the two theories, the obligation to lead a moral life ; and to this sensible view of their functions the bishops and clergy had in fact gradually arrived in the last century, when the revival of what is called earnestness, first in the form of Evangelicalism, and then of Anglo-Catholicism, awoke again the old controversies.

To a man of fervid temperament suddenly convinced of sin, incapable of being satisfied with ambiguous answers to questions which mean life or death to him, the Church of England has little to say. If he is quiet and reasonable, he finds in it all that he desires. En- thusiastic ages and enthusiastical temperaments demand something more complete and consistent. The clergy under the Long Parliament caught partially the tone of the prevailing spirit. The reading of the 'Book of Sports' had been interdicted, and from their pulpits they lectured their congregations on the ungodliness of the Sabbath amusements. But the congregations were slow to listen, and the sports went on.

One Sunday morning, when Bunyan was at church with his wife, a sermon was delivered on this subject. It seemed to be especially addressed to himself, and it much affected him. He shook off the impression, and after dinner he went as usual to the green. He was on the point of striking at a ball when the thought rushed across his mind, Wilt thou leave thy sins and go to Heaven, or have thy sins and go to hell ? He looked up. The reflection of his own emotion was before him in visible form. He imagined that he saw Christ himself looking down at him from the sky. But he concluded that it was too late for him to repent. He was past pardon. He was sure to be damned, and he might as well be damned for many sins as for few. Sin at all events was pleasant, the only pleasant thing that he knew, therefore he would take his fill of it. The sin was the game, and nothing but the game. He continued to play, but the Puritan sensitiveness had taken hold of him. An artificial offence had become a real offence when his conscience was wounded by it. He was reckless and desperate.

'This temptation of the devil,' he says, ' is more usual among poor creatures than many are aware of. It continued with me about a month or more ; but one day as I was standing at a neighbour's shop-window, and there cursing and swearing after my wonted manner, there sate within the woman of the house and heard me, who, though she was a loose and ungodly wretch, protested that I swore and cursed at such a rate that she trembled to hear me. I was able to spoil all the youths in a whole town. At this reproof I was silenced and put to secret shame, and that too, as I thought, before the God of Heaven. I stood hanging down my head and wishing that I might be a little child that my father might learn me to speak without this wicked sin of swearing, for, thought I, I am so accustomed to it that it is vain to think of a reformation.'

These words have been sometimes taken as a reflection on Bunyan's own father, as if he had not sufficiently checked the first symptoms of a bad habit. If this was so, too much may be easily made of it. The language in the homes of ignorant workmen is seldom select. They have not a large vocabulary, and the words which they use do not mean what they seem to mean. But so sharp and sudden remorse speaks remarkably for Bunyan himself. At this time he could have been barely twenty years old, and already he was quick to see when he was doing wrong, to be sorry for it, and to wish that he could do better. Vain the effort seemed to him, yet from that moment 'he did leave off swearing to his own great wonder,' and he found 'that he could speak better and more pleasantly than he did before.'

It lies in the nature of human advance on the road of improvement, that, whatever be a man's occupation, be it handicraft, or art, or knowledge, or moral conquest of self, at each forward step which he takes he grows more conscious of his shortcomings. It is thus with his whole career, and those who rise highest are least satisfied with themselves. Very simply Bunyan tells the story of his progress. On his outward history, on his business and his fortunes with it, he is totally silent. Worldly interests were not worth mentioning. He is solely occupied with his rescue from spiritual perdition. Soon after he had profited by the woman's rebuke, he fell in 'with a poor man that made profession of religion and talked pleasantly of the Scriptures.' Earnestness in such matters was growing common among English labourers. Under his new friend's example, Bunyan 'betook him to the Bible, and began to take great pleasure in reading it,' but especially, as he admits frankly (and most people's experience will have been the same), 'especially the historical part; for as for St. Paul's Epistles and Scriptures of that nature, he could not away with them, being as yet ignorant of the corruption of his nature, or of the want and worth of Jesus Christ to save him.'

Not as yet understanding these mysteries, he set himself to reform his life. He became strict with himself in word and deed. 'He set the Commandments before him for his way to Heaven.' 'He thought if he could but keep them pretty well he should have comfort.' If now and then he broke one of them, he suffered in conscience; he repented of his fault, he made good resolutions for the future and struggled to carry them out. 'His neighbours took him to be a new man, and marvelled at the alteration.' Pleasure of any kind, even the most innocent, he considered to be a snare to him, and he abandoned it; he had been fond of dancing, but he gave it up. Music and singing he parted with, though it distressed him to leave them. Of all amusements, that in which he had most delighted had been in ringing the bells in Elstow church tower. With his bells he could not part all at once. He would no longer ring himself: but when his friends were enjoying themselves with the ropes, he could not help going now and then to the tower door to look on and listen; but he feared at last that the steeple might fall upon him and kill him. We call such scruples in these days exaggerated and fantastic. We are no longer in danger ourselves of suffering from similar emotions. Whether we are the better for having got rid of them, will be seen in the future history of our race.

Notwithstanding his struggles and his sacrifices, Bunyan found that they did not bring him the peace which he expected. A man can change his outward conduct, but if he is in earnest he comes in sight of other features in himself which he cannot change so easily; the meannesses, the paltrinesses, the selfishnesses which haunt him in spite of himself, which start out upon him at moments the most unlooked for, which taint the best of his actions and make him loathe and hate himself. Bunyan's life was now for so young a person a model of correctness; but he had no sooner brought his actions straight than he discovered that he was admiring and approving of himself.

No situation is more humiliating, none brings with it a
feeling of more entire hopelessness. 'All this while,' he
says, 'I knew not Christ, nor grace, nor faith, nor hope,
and had I then died my state had been most fearful. I
was but a poor painted hypocrite, going about to establish
my own righteousness.'

Like his own Pilgrim, he had the burden on his back of
his conscious unworthiness. How was he to be rid of it?

'One day in a street in Bedford, as he was at work in
his calling, he fell in with three or four poor women sitting at a door in the sun talking about the things of God.'
He was himself at that time 'a brisk talker' about the
matters of religion, and he joined these women. Their
expressions were wholly unintelligible to him. 'They
were speaking of the wretchedness of their own hearts, of
their unbelief, of their miserable state. They did con-
temn, slight, and abhor their own righteousness as filthy
and insufficient to do them any good. They spoke of a
new birth and of the work of God in their hearts, which
comforted and strengthened them against the temptations
of the Devil.'

The language of the poor women has lost its old
meaning. They themselves, if they were alive, would not
use it any longer. The conventional phrases of Evangelical Christianity ring untrue in a modern ear like a
cracked bell. We have grown so accustomed to them as
a cant, that we can hardly believe that they ever stood
for sincere convictions. Yet these forms were once alive
with the profoundest of all moral truths; a truth not of
a narrow theology, but which lies at the very bottom of
the well, at the fountain-head of human morality; namely,
that a man who would work out his salvation must cast
out self, though he rend his heart-strings in doing it; not

love of self-indulgence only, but self-applause, self-confidence, self-conceit and vanity, desire or expectation of
reward; self in all the subtle ingenuities with which it
winds about the soul.   In one dialect or another, he
must recognise that he is himself a poor creature not
worth thinking of, or he will not take the first step towards excellence in any single thing which he undertakes.

Bunyan left the women and went about his work, but
their talk went with him. 'He was greatly affected.'
'He saw that he wanted the true tokens of a godly man.'
He sought them out and spoke with them again and again.
He could not stay away; and the more he went the more
he questioned his condition.

'I found two things,' he says, 'at which I did sometimes marvel, considering what a blind ungodly wretch
but just before I was; one a great softness and tenderness
of heart, which caused me to fall under the conviction of
what, by Scripture, they asserted; the other a great
bending of my mind to a continual meditating on it. My
mind was now like a horse-leech at the vein, still crying
Give, give; so fixed on eternity and on the kingdom of
heaven (though I knew but little), that neither pleasure,
nor profit, nor persuasion, nor threats could loosen it or
make it let go its hold. It is in very deed a certain
truth; it would have been then as difficult for me to have
taken my mind from heaven to earth, as I have found it
often since to get it from earth to heaven.'

Ordinary persons who are conscious of trying to do
right, who resist temptations, are sorry when they slip,
and determine to be more on their guard for the future,
are well contented with the condition which they have
reached.   They are respectable, they are right-minded in
common things, they fulfil their every-day duties to their

families and to society with a sufficiency for which the
world speaks well of them, as indeed it ought to speak;
and they themselves acquiesce in the world's verdict.
Any passionate agitation about the state of their souls
they consider unreal and affected. Such men may be
amiable in private life, good neighbours, and useful
citizens; but be their talents what they may, they
could not write a 'Pilgrim's Progress,' or ever reach the
Delectable Mountains, or even be conscious that such
mountains exist.

Bunyan was on the threshold of the higher life. He
knew that he was a very poor creature. He longed to
rise to something better. He was a mere ignorant, un-
taught mechanic. He had not been to school with Aristotle and Plato. He could not help himself or lose
himself in the speculations of poets and philosophers. He
had only the Bible, and studying the Bible he found that
the wonder-working power in man's nature was Faith.
Faith! What was it? What did it mean? Had he faith?
He was but 'a poor sot,' and yet he thought that he could
not be wholly without it. The Bible told him that if he
had faith as a grain of mustard seed, he could work
miracles. He did not understand Oriental metaphors;
here was a simple test which could be at once applied.

'One day,' he writes, 'as I was between Elstow and
Bedford, the temptation was hot upon me to try if I had
faith by doing some miracle. I must say to the puddles
that were in the horse-pads, " be dry," and truly at one
time I was agoing to say so indeed. But just as I was
about to speak, the thought came into my mind : Go un
der yonder hedge first and pray that God would make
you able. But when I had concluded to pray, this came
hot upon me, that if I prayed and came again and tried

to do it, and yet did nothing notwithstanding, then be
sure I had no faith but was a castaway and lost. Nay,
thought I, if it be so, I will never try it yet, but will
stay a little longer. Thus was I tossed between the
Devil and my own ignorance, and so perplexed at some
times that I could not tell what to do.'

Common sense will call this disease, and will think
impatiently that the young tinker would have done better
to attend to his business. But it must be observed that
Bunyan was attending to his business, toiling all the
while with grimed hands over his pots and kettles. No
one ever complained that the pots and kettles were ill-
mended. It was merely that being simple-minded, he
found in his Bible that besides earning his bread he had
to save or lose his soul. Having no other guide he took
its words literally, and the directions puzzled him.

He grew more and more unhappy—more lowly in his
own eyes—

   ' Wishing him like to those more rich in hope '—

like the women who were so far beyond him on the
heavenly road. He was a poet without knowing it, and
his gifts only served to perplex him further. His speculations assumed bodily forms which he supposed to be
actual visions. He saw his poor friends sitting on the
sunny side of a high mountain refreshing themselves in
the warmth, while he was shivering in frost and snow
and mist. The mountain was surrounded by a wall,
through which he tried to pass, and searched long in vain
for an opening through it. At last he found one, very
straight and narrow, through which he struggled after
desperate efforts. 'It showed him,' he said, 'that none
could enter into life but those who were in downright
earnest, and unless they left the wicked world behind

them, for here was only room for body and soul, but not for body and soul and sin.' The vision brought him no comfort, for it passed away and left him still on the wrong side : a little comfortable self-conceit would have set him at rest. But, like all real men, Bunyan had the worst opinion of himself. He looked at his Bible again. He found that he must be elected. Was he elected ? He could as little tell as whether he had faith. He knew that he longed to be elected, but 'the Scripture trampled on his desire,' for it said, 'It is not of him that willeth, or of him that runneth, but of God that sheweth mercy ; ' therefore, unless God had chosen him his labour was in vain. The Devil saw his opportunity ; the Devil among his other attributes must have possessed that of omni-presence, for whenever any human soul was in straits, he was personally at hand to take advantage of it.

'It may be that you are not elected,' the tempter said to Bunyan. 'It may be so indeed,' thought he. 'Why then,' said Satan, 'you had as good leave off and strive no farther ; for if indeed you should not be elected and chosen of God, there is no talk of your being saved.'

A comforting text suggested itself. 'Look at the generations of old ; did any ever trust in the Lord and was confounded ? ' But these exact words, unfortunately, were only to be found in the Apocrypha. And there was a further distressing possibility, which has occurred to others besides Bunyan. Perhaps the day of grace was passed. It came on him one day as he walked in the country that perhaps those good people in Bedford were all that the Lord would save in those parts, and that he came too late for the blessing. True, Christ had said, 'Compel them to come in, for yet there is room.' It might be 'that when Christ spoke those words,' He was thinking of him—him among the rest that he had chosen, and had meant to encourage him. But Bunyan was too simply modest to gather comfort from such aspiring thoughts. He desired to be converted, craved for it, longed for it with all his heart and soul. ' Could it have been gotten for gold,' he said, ' what would I not have given for it. Had I had a whole world it had all gone ten thousand times over for this, that my soul might have been in a converted state. But, oh! I was made sick by that saying of Christ : " He called to Him whom He would, and they came to Him." I feared He would not call me.'

Election, conversion, day of grace, coming to Christ, have been pawed and fingered by unctuous hands for now two hundred years. The bloom is gone from the flower. The plumage, once shining with hues direct from heaven, is soiled and bedraggled. The most solemn of all realities have been degraded into the passwords of technical theology. In Bunyan's day, in camp and council chamber, in High Courts of Parliament, and among the poor drudges in English villages, they were still radiant with spiritual meaning. The dialect may alter; but if man is more than a brief floating bubble on the eternal river of time; if there be really an immortal part of him which need not perish; and if his business on earth is to save it from perishing, he will still try to pierce the mountain barrier. He will still find the work as hard as Bunyan found it. We live in days of progress and enlightenment; nature on a hundred sides has unlocked her storehouses of knowledge. But she has furnished no ' open sesame' to bid the mountain gate fly wide which leads to conquest of self. There is still no passage there for ' body and soul and sin.'

CHAPTER III.

GRACE ABOUNDING.

THE women in Bedford, to whom Bunyan had opened his mind, had been naturally interested in him. Young and rough as he was, he could not have failed to impress anyone who conversed with him with a sense that he was a remarkable person. They mentioned him to Mr. Gifford, the minister of the Baptist Church at Bedford. John Gifford had, at the beginning of the Civil War, been a loose young officer in the king's army. He had been taken prisoner when engaged in some exploit which was contrary to the usages of war. A court-martial had sentenced him to death, and he was to have been shot in a few hours, when he broke out of his prison with his sister's help, and, after various adventures, settled at Bedford as a doctor. The near escape had not sobered him. He led a disorderly life, drinking and gambling, till the loss of a large sum of money startled him into seriousness. In the language of the time he became convinced of sin, and joined the Baptists, the most thoroughgoing and consistent of all the Protestant sects. If the Sacrament of Baptism is not a magical form, but is a personal act, in which the baptised person devotes himself to Christ's service, to baptise children at an age when they cannot understand what they are doing may well seem irrational and even impious.

Gifford, who was now the head of the Baptist community in the town, invited Bunyan to his house, and explained the causes of his distress to him. He was a lost sinner. It was true that he had parted with his old faults, and was leading a new life. But his heart was unchanged; his past offences stood in record against him. He was still under the wrath of God, miserable in his position, and therefore miserable in mind. He must become sensible of his lost state, and lay hold of the only remedy, or there was no hope for him.

There was no difficulty in convincing Bunyan that he was in a bad way. He was too well aware of it already. In a work of fiction, the conviction would be followed immediately by consoling grace. In the actual experience of a living human soul, the medicine operates less pleasantly.

' I began,' he says, ' to see something of the vanity and inward wretchedness of my wicked heart, for as yet I knew no great matter therein. But now it began to be discovered unto me, and to work for wickedness as it never did before. Lusts and corruptions would strongly put themselves forth within me in wicked thoughts and desires which I did not regard before. Whereas, before, my soul was full of longing after God; now my heart began to hanker after every foolish vanity.'

Constitutions differ. Mr. Gifford's treatment, if it was ever good for any man, was too sharp for Bunyan. The fierce acid which had been poured into his wounds set them all festering again. He frankly admits that he was now farther from conversion than before. His heart, do what he would, refused to leave off desiring forbidden pleasures,

and while this continued, he supposed that he was still
under the law, and must perish by it. He compared
himself to the child who, as he was being brought to
Christ, was thrown down by the devil and wallowed foaming. A less healthy nature might have been destroyed
by these artificially created and exaggerated miseries. He
supposed he was given over to unbelief and wickedness,
and yet he relates with touching simplicity :—

'As to the act of sinning I was never more tender
than now. I durst not take up a pin or a stick, though
but so big as a straw, for my conscience now was sore and
would smart at every touch. I could not tell how to
speak my words for fear I should misplace them.'

But the care with which he watched his conduct
availed him nothing. He was on a morass ' that shook if
he did but stir,' and he was 'there left both of God and
Christ and the Spirit, and of all good things.' Behind
him lay the faults of his childhood and youth, every one
of which he believed to be recorded against him. Within
were his disobedient inclinations, which he conceived to
be the presence of the Devil in his heart. If he was to
be presented clean of stain before God he must have a perfect righteousness which was to be found only in Christ,
and Christ had rejected him. ' My original and inward
pollution,' he writes, 'was my plague and my affliction.
I was more loathsome in my own eyes than was a toad, and
I thought I was so in God's eyes too. I thought every
one had a better heart than I had. I could have changed
heart with anybody. I thought none but the Devil himself could equal me for inward wickedness and pollution.
Sure, thought I, I am given up to the Devil and to a
reprobate mind ; and thus I continued for a long while,
even for some years together.'

And all the while the world went on so quietly; these things over which Bunyan was so miserable not seeming to trouble anyone except himself; and, as if they had no existence except on Sundays and in pious talk. Old people were hunting after the treasures of this life, as if they were never to leave the earth. Professors of religion complained when they lost fortune or health; what were fortune and health to the awful possibilities which lay beyond the grave? To Bunyan the future life of Christianity was a reality as certain as the next day's sunrise; and he could have been happy on bread and water if he could have felt himself prepared to enter it. Every created being seemed better off than he was. He was sorry that God had made him a man. He 'blessed the condition of the birds, beasts, and fishes, for they had not a sinful nature. They were not obnoxious to the wrath of God. They were not to go to hell-fire after death.' He recalled the texts which spoke of Christ and forgiveness. He tried to persuade himself that Christ cared for him. He could have talked of Christ's love and mercy 'even to the very crows which sate on the ploughed land before him.' But he was too sincere to satisfy himself with formulas and phrases. He could not, he would not, profess to be convinced that things would go well with him when he was not convinced. Cold spasms of doubt laid hold of him—doubts, not so much of his own salvation, as of the truth of all that he had been taught to believe; and the problem had to be fought and grappled with, which lies in the intellectual nature of every genuine man, whether he be an Æschylus or a Shakespeare, or a poor working Bedfordshire mechanic. No honest soul can look out upon the world and see it as it really is, without the question rising in him whether there be any God that

governs it at all. No one can accept the popular notion
of heaven and hell as actually true, without being as terrified as Bunyan was. We go on as we do, and attend to
our business and enjoy ourselves, because the words have
no real meaning to us. Providence in its kindness leaves
most of us unblessed or uncursed with natures of too fine
a fibre.

Bunyan was hardly dealt with. ' Whole floods of
blasphemies,' he says, ' against God, Christ, and the
Scriptures were poured upon my spirit ; questions against
the very being of God and of his only beloved Son, as
whether there was in truth a God or Christ, or no, and
whether the Holy Scriptures were not rather a fable and
cunning story than the holy and pure Word of God.'

' How can you tell,' the tempter whispered, ' but that
the Turks have as good a Scripture to prove their
Mahomet the Saviour, as we have to prove our Jesus is ?
Could I think that so many tens of thousands in so many
countries and kingdoms should be without the knowledge
of the right way to heaven, if there were indeed a heaven,
and that we who lie in a corner of the earth, should alone
be blessed therewith. Every one doth think his own religion the rightest, both Jews, Moors, and Pagans ; and
how if all our faith, and Christ, and Scripture should be
but " a think so " too.' St. Paul spoke positively. Bunyan
saw shrewdly that on St. Paul the weight of the whole
Christian theory really rested. But ' how could he tell
but that S. Paul, being a subtle and cunning man, might
give himself up to deceive with strong delusions ?' ' He
was carried away by such thoughts as by a whirlwind.'

His belief in the active agency of the Devil in human
affairs, of which he supposed that he had witnessed in-
stances, was no doubt a great help to him. If he could

have imagined that his doubts or misgivings had been suggested by a desire for truth, they would have been harder
to bear.   More than ever he was convinced that he was
possessed by the devil.   He 'compared himself to a child
carried off by a gipsy.'   ' Kick sometimes I did,' he says,
' and scream, and cry, but yet I was as bound in the
wings of temptation, and the wind would bear me
away.'   ' I blessed the dog and toad, and counted the
condition of everything that God had made far better
than this dreadful state of mine.   The dog or horse had
no soul to perish under the everlasting weight of hell for
sin, as mine was like to do.'

Doubts about revelation and the truth of Scripture
were more easy to encounter then than they are at
present.   Bunyan was protected by want of learning, and
by a powerful predisposition to find the objections against
the credibility of the Gospel history to be groundless.
Critical investigation had not as yet analysed the historical construction of the sacred books, and scepticism,
as he saw it in people round him, did actually come
from the devil, that is from a desire to escape the
moral restraints of religion.   The wisest, noblest, best
instructed men in England, at that time regarded the
Bible as an authentic communication from God, and as
the only foundation for law and civil society.   The masculine sense and strong modest intellect of Bunyan
ensured his acquiescence in an opinion so powerfully supported.   Fits of uncertainty recurred even to the end of
his life ; it must be so with men who are honestly in
earnest ; but his doubts were of course only intermittent,
and his judgment was in the main satisfied that the Bible
was, as he had been taught, the Word of God.   This,
however, helped him little ; for in the Bible he read his

own condemnation. The weight which pressed him down was the sense of his unworthiness. What was he that God should care for him? He fancied that he heard God saying to the angels, ' This poor, simple wretch doth hanker after me, as if I had nothing to do with my mercy but to bestow it on such as he. Poor fool, how art thou deceived! It is not for such as thee to have favour with the Highest.'

Miserable as he was, he clung to his misery as the one link which connected him with the object of his longings. If he had no hope of heaven, he was at least distracted that he must lose it. He was afraid of dying, yet he was still more afraid of continuing to live; lest the impression should wear away through time, and occupation and other interests should turn his heart away to the world, and thus his wounds might cease to pain him.

Readers of the ' Pilgrim's Progress ' sometimes ask with wonder, why, after Christian had been received into the narrow gate, and had been set forward upon his way, so many trials and dangers still lay before him. The answer is simply that Christian was a pilgrim, that the journey of life still lay before him, and at every step temptations would meet him in new, unexpected shapes. St. Anthony in his hermitage was beset by as many fiends as had ever troubled him when in the world. Man's spiritual existence is like the flight of a bird in the air; he is sustained only by effort, and when he ceases to exert himself he falls. There are intervals, however, of comparative calm, and to one of these the storm-tossed Bunyan was now approaching. He had passed through the Slough of Despond. He had gone astray after Mr. Legality, and the rocks had almost overwhelmed him. Evangelist now found him and put him right again, and

he was to be allowed a breathing space at the Interpreter's
house.   As he was at his ordinary daily work his mind
was restlessly busy.   Verses of Scripture came into his
head, sweet while present, but like Peter's sheet caught
up again into heaven.   We may have heard all our lives
of Christ.   Words and ideas with which we have been
familiar from childhood are trodden into paths as barren
as sand.   Suddenly, we know not how, the meaning
flashes upon us.   The seed has found its way into some
corner of our minds where it can germinate.   The shell
breaks, the cotyledons open, and the plant of faith is alive.
So it was now to be with Bunyan.

   ' One day,' he says, ' as I was travelling into the
country, musing on the wickedness of my heart, and considering the enmity that was in me to God, the Scripture came into my mind, "He hath made peace through
the blood of His cross."   I saw that the justice of God
and my sinful soul could embrace and kiss each other.   I
was ready to swoon, not with grief and trouble, but with
solid joy and peace.'   Everything became clear : the
Gospel history, the birth, the life, the death of the
Saviour ; how gently he gave himself to be nailed on the
cross for his (Bunyan's) sins.   ' I saw Him in the spirit,'
he goes on, ' a Man on the right hand of the Father,
pleading for me, and have seen the manner of His coming
from Heaven to judge the world with glory.'

   The sense of guilt which had so oppressed him was
now a key to the mystery.   ' God,' he says, ' suffered me
to be afflicted with temptations concerning these things,
and then revealed them to me.'   He was crushed to
the ground by the thought of his wickedness ; ' the Lord
showed him the death of Christ, and lifted the weight
away.'

Now he thought he had a personal evidence from
Heaven that he was really saved. Before this, he had
lain trembling at the mouth of hell; now he was so far
away from it that he could scarce tell where it was. He
fell in at this time with a copy of Luther's commentary
on the Epistle to the Galatians, 'so old that it was like
to fall to pieces.' Bunyan found in it the exact counter-
part of his own experience: 'of all the books that he
had ever met with, it seemed to him the most fit for a
wounded conscience.'

Everything was supernatural with him : when a bad
thought came into his mind, it was the devil that put it
there. These breathings of peace he regarded as the immediate voice of his Savour. Alas ! the respite was but
short. He had hoped that his troubles were over, when
the tempter came back upon him in the most extraordinary form which he had yet assumed. Bunyan had himself left the door open ; the evil spirits could only enter
'Mansoul' through the owner's negligence, but once in,
they could work their own wicked will. How it happened will be told afterwards. The temptation itself
must be described first. Never was a nature more per-
versely ingenious in torturing itself.

He had gained Christ, as he called it. He was now
tempted 'to sell and part with this most blessed Christ,
to exchange Him for the things of this life—for anything.'
If there had been any real prospect of worldly advantage
before Bunyan, which he could have gained by abandon-
ing his religious profession, the words would have had a
meaning ; but there is no hint or trace of any prospect of
the kind ; nor in Bunyan's position could there have
been. The temptation, as he called it, was a freak of
fancy : fancy resenting the minuteness with which he

watched his own emotions. And yet he says, 'It lay upon me for a year, and did follow me so continually that I was not rid of it one day in a month, sometimes not an hour in many days together, unless when I was asleep. I could neither eat my food, stoop for a pin, chop a stick, or cast my eye to look on this or that, but still the temptation would come, "Sell Christ for this, sell Him for that! Sell Him! Sell Him!"'

He had been haunted before with a notion that he was under a spell; that he had been fated to commit the unpardonable sin; and he was now thinking of Judas, who had been admitted to Christ's intimacy, and had then betrayed him. Here it was before him—the very thing which he had so long dreaded. If his heart did but consent for a moment, the deed was done. His doom had overtaken him. He wrestled with the thought as it rose, thrust it from him 'with his hands and elbows,' body and mind convulsed together in a common agony. As fast as the destroyer said, 'Sell Him,' Bunyan said, 'I will not; I will not; I will not, not for thousands, thousands, thousands of worlds!' One morning as he lay in his bed, the voice came again, and would not be driven away. Bunyan fought against it, till he was out of breath. He fell back exhausted, and without conscious action of his will, the fatal sentence passed through his brain, 'Let Him go if He will.'

That the 'selling Christ' was a bargain in which he was to lose all and receive nothing is evident from the form in which he was overcome. Yet if he had gained a fortune by fraud or forgery, he could not have been more certain that he had destroyed himself.

Satan had won the battle, and he, 'as a bird shot from a tree, had fallen into guilt and despair.' He got out of bed, 'and went moping into the fields,' where he wandered for two hours, 'as a man bereft of life, and now past recovering,' 'bound over to eternal punishment.' He shrank under the hedges, 'in guilt and sorrow, bemoaning the hardness of his fate.' In vain the words now came back that had so comforted him, 'The blood of Christ cleanseth from all sin.' They had no application to him. He had acquired his birthright, but, like Esau, he had sold it, and could not any more find place for repentance. True it was said that 'all manner of sins and blasphemies should be forgiven unto men,' but only such sins and blasphemies as had been committed in the natural state. Bunyan had received grace, and after receiving it, had sinned against the Holy Ghost.

It was done, and nothing could undo it. David had received grace, and had committed murder and adultery after it. But murder and adultery, bad as they might be, were only transgressions of the law of Moses. Bunyan had sinned against the Mediator himself, 'he had sold his Saviour.' One sin, and only one there was which could not be pardoned, and he had been guilty of it. Peter had sinned against grace, and even after he had been warned. Peter, however, had but denied his Master. Bunyan had sold him. He was no David or Peter, he was Judas. It was very hard. Others naturally as bad as he had been saved. Why had he been picked out to be made a Son of Perdition? A Judas! Was there any point in which he was better than Judas? Judas had sinned with deliberate purpose: he 'in a fearful hurry,' and 'against prayer and striving.' But there might be more ways than one of committing the unpardonable sin, and there might be degrees of it. It was a dreadful condition. The old doubts came back.

'I was now ashamed,' he says, 'that I should be like
such an ugly man as Judas. I thought how loathsome I
should be to all the saints at the Day of Judgment. I
was tempted to content myself by receiving some false
opinion, as that there should be no such thing as the Day
of Judgment, that we should not rise again, that sin was
no such grievous thing, the tempter suggesting that if
these things should be indeed true, yet to believe otherwise would yield me ease for the present. If I must
perish, I need not torment myself beforehand.'

Judas! Judas! was now for ever before his eyes.
So identified he was with Judas that he felt at times as
if his breastbone was bursting. A mark like Cain's was
on him. In vain he searched again through the catalogue
of pardoned sinners. Manasseh had consulted wizards
and familiar spirits. Manasseh had burnt his children in
the fire to devils. He had found mercy; but, alas!
Manasseh's sins had nothing of the nature of selling the
Saviour. To have sold the Saviour 'was a sin bigger
than the sins of a country, of a kingdom, or of the whole
world—not all of them together could equal it.'

His brain was overstrained, it will be said. Very
likely. It is to be remembered, however, who and what
he was, and that he had overstrained it in his eagerness to
learn what he conceived his Maker to wish him to be—a
form of anxiety not common in this world. The cure was
as remarkable as the disorder. One day he was 'in a
good man's shop,' still 'afflicting himself with self-
abhorrence,' when something seemed to rush in through an
open window, and he heard a voice saying, 'Didst ever
refuse to be justified by the blood of Christ?' Bunyan
shared the belief of his time. He took the system of
things as the Bible represented it; but his strong com-

mon sense put him on his guard against being easily credulous. He thought at the time that the voice was supernatural. After twenty years he said modestly that he 'could not make a judgment of it.' The effect, any way, was as if an angel had come to him and had told him that there was still hope. Hapless as his condition was, he might still pray for mercy, and might possibly find it. He tried to pray, and found it very hard. The devil whispered again that God was tired of him; God wanted to be rid of him and his importunities, and had, there-fore, allowed him to commit this particular sin that he might hear no more of him. He remembered Esau, and thought that this might be too true: 'the saying about Esau was a flaming sword barring the way of the tree of life to him.' Still he would not give in. 'I can but die,' he said to himself, 'and if it must be so, it shall be said that such an one died at the feet of Christ in prayer.'

He was torturing himself with illusions. Most of the saints in the Catholic Calendar have done the same. The most remorseless philosopher can hardly refuse a certain admiration for this poor uneducated village lad struggling so bravely in the theological spider's web. The 'Pro-fessors' could not comfort him, having never experienced similar distresses in their own persons. He consulted 'an Antient Christian,' telling him that he feared that he had sinned against the Holy Ghost. The Antient Christian answered gravely that he thought so too. The devil having him at advantage, began to be witty with him. The devil suggested that as he had offended the second or third Person of the Trinity, he had better pray the Father to mediate for him with Christ and the Holy Spirit. Then the devil took another turn. Christ, he said, was

really sorry for Bunyan, but his case was beyond remedy.
Bunyan's sin was so peculiar, that it was not of the
nature of those for which He had bled and died, and had
not, therefore, been laid to His charge. To justify Bunyan
he must come down and die again, and that was not to be
thought of. 'Oh!' exclaimed the unfortunate victim,
'the unthought-of imaginations, frights, fears, and terrors, that are effected by a thorough application of guilt
(to a spirit) that is yielded to desperation. This is the
man that hath his dwelling among the tombs.'

Sitting in this humour on a settle in the street at Bedford, he was pondering over his fearful state. The sun
in heaven seemed to grudge its light to him. 'The stones
in the street and the tiles on the houses did bend themselves against him.' Each crisis in Bunyan's mind is
always framed in the picture of some spot where it occurred. He was crying 'in the bitterness of his soul,
How can God comfort such a wretch as I am?' As before, in the shop, a voice came in answer, 'This sin is not
unto death.' The first voice had brought him hope
which was almost extinguished; the second was a message
of life. The night was gone, and it was daylight. He
had come to the end of the Valley of the Shadow of
Death, and the spectres and the hobgoblins which had
jibbered at him suddenly all vanished. A moment before
he had supposed that he was out of reach of pardon, that
he had no right to pray, no right to repent, or, at least,
that neither prayer nor repentance could profit him. If
his sin was not to death, then he was on the same ground
as other sinners. If they might pray, he might pray,
and might look to be forgiven on the same terms. He
still saw that his 'selling Christ' had been 'most bar-
barous,' but despair was followed by an extravagance, no

less unbounded, of gratitude, when he felt that Christ would pardon even this.

'Love and affection for Christ,' he says, 'did work at this time such a strong and hot desire of revengement upon myself for the abuse I had done to Him, that, to speak as then I thought, had I had a thousand gallons of blood in my veins, I could freely have spilt it all at the command of my Lord and Saviour. The tempter told me it was vain to pray. Yet, thought I, I will pray. But, said the tempter, your sin is unpardonable. Well, said I, I will pray. It is no boot, said he. Yet, said I, I will pray : so I went to prayer, and I uttered words to this effect : Lord, Satan tells me that neither Thy mercy nor Christ's blood is sufficient to save my soul. Lord, shall I honour Thee most by believing that Thou wilt and canst, or him, by believing that Thou neither wilt nor canst ? Lord, I would fain honour Thee by believing that Thou wilt and canst. As I was there before the Lord, the Scripture came, Oh ! man, great is thy faith, even as if one had clapped me on the back.'

The waves had not wholly subsided ; but we need not follow the undulations any farther. It is enough that after a 'conviction of sin,' considerably deeper than most people find necessary for themselves, Bunyan had come to realise what was meant by salvation in Christ, according to the received creed of the contemporary Protestant world. The intensity of his emotions arose only from the completeness with which he believed it. Man had sinned, and by sin was made a servant of the devil. His redemption was a personal act of the Saviour towards each individual sinner. In the Atonement Christ had before him each separate person whom he designed to save, blotting out his offences, however heinous they

E

might be, and recording in place of them his own perfect obedience. Each reconciled sinner in return regarded
Christ's sufferings as undergone immediately for himself,
and gratitude for that great deliverance enabled and
obliged him to devote his strength and soul thenceforward to God's service. In the seventeenth century, all
earnest English Protestants held this belief. In the nine-
teenth century, most of us repeat the phrases of this
belief, and pretend to hold it. We think we hold it. We
are growing more cautious, perhaps, with our definitions.
We suspect that there may be mysteries in God's nature
and methods which we cannot fully explain. The outlines of 'the scheme of salvation' are growing indistinct;
and we see it through a gathering mist. Yet the essence
of it will remain true whether we recognise it or not.
While man remains man he will do things which he
ought not to do. He will leave undone things which he
ought to do. To will, may be present with him; but how
to perform what he wills, he will never fully know, and
he will still hate 'the body of death' which he feels
clinging to him. He will try to do better. When he
falls he will struggle to his feet again. He will climb
and climb on the hill side, though he never reaches the
top, and knows that he can never reach it. His life will
be a failure, which he will not dare to offer as a fit
account of himself, or as worth a serious regard. Yet
he will still hope that he will not be wholly cast away,
when after his sleep in death he wakes again.

Now, says Bunyan, there remained only the hinder
part of the tempest. Heavenly voices continued to encourage him. 'As I was passing in the field,' he goes on,
'I heard the sentence, thy righteousness is in heaven; and
methought I saw, with the eyes of my soul, Jesus Christ

at God's right hand, there I say, as my righteousness, so
that wherever I was, or whatever I was doing, God could
not say of me He wants my righteousness, for that was
just before Him. Now did my chains fall off my legs
indeed. I was loosed from my affliction and irons; my
temptations also fled away, so that from that time those
dreadful Scriptures of God left off to trouble me. Now
went I home rejoicing for the grace and love of God.
Christ of God is made unto us wisdom and righteousness,
and sanctification, and redemption. I now lived very
sweetly at peace with God through Christ. Oh! methought, Christ, Christ! There was nothing but Christ
before my eyes. I was not now only looking upon this
and the other benefits of Christ apart, as of His blood,
burial, and resurrection, but considered Him as a whole
Christ. All those graces that were now green in me
were yet but like those cracked groats and fourpence half-
pennies which rich men carry in their purses, while their
gold is in their trunks at home. Oh! I saw my gold
was in my trunk at home in Christ my Lord and Saviour.
The Lord led me into the mystery of union with the Son
of God, that I was joined to Him, that I was flesh of His
flesh. If He and I were one, His righteousness was
mine, His merits mine, His victory mine. Now I could
see myself in heaven and earth at once; in heaven by my
Christ, though on earth by my body and person. Christ
was that common and public person in whom the whole
body of His elect are always to be considered and reckoned.
We fulfilled the law by Him, died by Him, rose from the
dead by Him, got the victory over sin and death, the devil
and hell by Him. I had cause to say, Praise ye the Lord.
Praise God in His sanctuary.'

CHAPTER IV.

CALL TO THE MINISTRY.

THE Pilgrim falls into the hands of Giant Despair because he has himself first strayed into Byepath Meadow. Bunyan found an explanation of his last convulsion in an act of unbelief, of which, on looking back, he perceived that he had been guilty. He had been delivered out of his first temptation. He had not been sufficiently on his guard against temptations that might come in the future. Nay, he had himself tempted God. His wife had been overtaken by a premature confinement, and was suffering acutely. It was at the time when Bunyan was exercised with questions about the truth of religion altogether. As the poor woman lay crying at his side, he had said mentally, 'Lord, if Thou wilt now remove this sad affliction from my wife, and cause that she be troubled no more therewith this night, then I shall know that Thou canst discern the more secret thoughts of the heart.' In a moment the pain ceased and she fell into a sleep which lasted till morning. Bunyan, though surprised at the time, forgot what had happened, till it rushed back upon his memory, when he had committed himself by a similar mental assent to selling Christ. He remembered the proof which had been given to him that God could and did discern his thoughts. God had discerned this second

thought also, and in punishing him for it had punished
him at the same time for the doubt which he had allowed
himself to feel. ' I should have believed His word,' he
said, ' and not have put an " if " upon the all-seeingness
of God.'

The suffering was over now, and he felt that it had
been infinitely beneficial to him. He understood better
the glory of God and of his Son. The Scriptures had
opened their secrets to him, and he had seen them to be
in very truth the keys of the kingdom of Heaven. Never
so clearly as after this ' temptation ' had he perceived ' the
heights of grace, and love, and mercy.' Two or three
times ' he had such strange apprehensions of the grace of
God as had amazed him.' The impression was so overpowering that if it had continued long ' it would have
rendered him incapable for business.' He joined his
friend Mr. Gifford's church. He was baptised in the
Ouse, and became a professed member of the Baptist congregation. Soon after, his mental conflict was entirely
over, and he had two quiet years of peace. Before a man
can use his powers to any purpose, he must arrive at some
conviction in which his intellect can acquiesce. ' Calm
yourself,' says Jean Paul; ' it is your first necessity. Be
a stoic if nothing else will serve.' Bunyan had not been
driven into stoicism. He was now restored to the possession of his faculties, and his remarkable ability was not
long in showing itself.

The first consequence of his mental troubles was an
illness. He had a cough which threatened to turn into
consumption. He thought it was all over with him, and
he was fixing his eyes ' on the heavenly Jerusalem and the
innumerable company of angels ; ' but the danger passed
off, and he became well and strong in mind and body,

Notwithstanding his various miseries, he had not neglected his business, and had indeed been specially successful. By the time that he was twenty-five years old
he was in a position considerably superior to that in
which he was born. 'God,' says a contemporary biographer, 'had increased his stores so that he lived in
great credit among his neighbours.' On May 13, 1653,
Bedfordshire sent an address to Cromwell approving the
dismissal of the Long Parliament, recognising Oliver himself as the Lord's instrument, and recommending the
county magistrates as fit persons to serve in the Assembly
which was to take its place. Among thirty-six names
attached to this document, appear those of Gifford and
Bunyan. This speaks for itself: he must have been at
least a householder and a person of consideration. It was
not, however, as a prosperous brazier that Bunyan was to
make his way. He had a gift of speech, which, in the
democratic congregation to which he belonged, could not
long remain hid. Young as he was, he had sounded the
depths of spiritual experience. Like Dante he had been
in hell—the popular hell of English Puritanism—and in
1655 he was called upon to take part in the 'ministry.'
He was modest, humble, shrinking. The minister when
he preached was, according to the theory, an instrument
uttering the words not of himself but of the Holy Spirit.
A man like Bunyan, who really believed this, might well
be alarmed. After earnest entreaty, however, ' he made
experiment of his powers ' in private, and it was at once
evident that, with the thing which these people meant by
inspiration, he was abundantly supplied. No such preacher
to the uneducated English masses was to be found within
the four seas. He says that he had no desire of vain
glory ; no one who has studied his character can suppose

that he had. He was a man of natural genius, who believed the Protestant form of Christianity to be completely
true. He knew nothing of philosophy, nothing of history,
nothing of literature. The doubts to which he acknowledged being without their natural food, had never presented themselves in a form which would have compelled
him to submit to remain uncertain. Doubt, as he had
felt it, was a direct enemy of morality and purity, and as
such he had fought with it and conquered it. Protestant
Christianity was true. All mankind were perishing unless they saw it to be true. This was his message; a
message—supposing him to have been right—of an importance so immeasurable that all else was nothing. He
was still 'afflicted with the fiery darts of the devil,' but
he saw that he must not bury his abilities. ' In fear and
trembling,' therefore, he set himself to the work, and ' did
according to his power preach the Gospel that God had
shewn him.'

' The Lord led him to begin where his Word began—
with sinners. This part of my work,' he says, ' I fulfilled
with a great sense, for the terrors of the law and guilt for
my transgressions lay heavy on my conscience. I preached
what I felt. I had been sent to my hearers as from the
dead. I went myself in chains to preach to them in chains,
and carried that fire in my own conscience that I persuaded them to beware of. I have gone full of guilt and
terror to the pulpit door ; God carried me on with a
strong hand, for neither guilt nor hell could take me off.'

Many of Bunyan's addresses remain in the form of
theological treatises, and that I may not have to return
to the subject, I shall give some account of them. His
doctrine was the doctrine of the best and strongest minds
in Europe. It had been believed by Luther, it had been

believed by Knox. It was believed at that moment by Oliver Cromwell as completely as by Bunyan himself. It was believed, so far as such a person could be said to believe anything, by the all-accomplished Leibnitz himself. Few educated people use the language of it now. In them it was a fire from heaven shining like a sun in a dark world. With us the fire has gone out; in the place of it we have but smoke and ashes, and the Evangelical mind in search of 'something deeper and truer than satisfied the last century,' is turning back to Catholic verities. What Bunyan had to say may be less than the whole truth : we shall scarcely find the still missing part of it in lines of thought which we have outgrown.

Bunyan preached wherever opportunity served—in woods, in barns, on village greens, or in town chapels. The substance of his sermons he revised and published. He began, as he said, with sinners, explaining the condition of men in the world. They were under the law, or they were under grace. Every person that came into the world was born under the law, and as such was bound, under pain of eternal damnation, to fulfil completely and continually every one of the Ten Commandments. The Bible said plainly, ' Cursed is every one that continueth not in all things which are written in the book of the law to do them.' ' The soul that sinneth it shall die.' The Ten Commandments extended into many more, and to fail in a single one was as fatal as to break them all. A man might go on for a long time, for sixty years perhaps, without falling. Bunyan does not mean that anyone really could do all this, but he assumes the possibility; yet he says if the man slipped once before he died, he would eternally perish. The law does not refer to words and actions only, but to thoughts and feelings. It followed a man in his prayers, and detected a wandering thought. It allowed no repentance to those who lived and died under it. If it was asked whether God could not pardon, as earthly judges pardon criminals, the answer was, that it is not the law which is merciful to the earthly offender but the magistrate. The law is an eternal principle. The magistrate may forgive a man without exacting satisfaction. The law knows no forgiveness. It can be as little changed as an axiom of mathematics. Repentance cannot undo the past. Let a man leave his sins and live as purely as an angel all the rest of his life, his old faults remain in the account against him, and his state is as bad as ever it was. God's justice once offended knows not pity or compassion, but runs on the offender like a lion and throws him into prison, there to lie to all eternity unless infinite satisfaction be given to it. And that satisfaction no son of Adam could possibly make.

This conception of Divine justice, not as a sentence of a judge, but as the action of an eternal law, is identical with Spinoza's. That every act involves consequences which cannot be separated from it, and may continue operative to eternity, is a philosophical position which is now generally admitted. Combined with the traditionary notions of a future judgment and punishment in hell, the recognition that there was a law in the case and that the law could not be broken, led to the frightful inference that each individual was liable to be kept alive and tortured through all eternity. And this, in fact, was the fate really in store for every human creature unless some extraordinary remedy could be found. Bunyan would allow no merit to anyone. He would not have it supposed that only the profane or grossly wicked were in danger from

the law. 'A man,' he says, 'may be turned from a vain,
loose, open, profane conversation and sinning against the
law, to a holy, righteous, religious life, and yet be under
the same state and as sure to be damned as the others
that are more profane and loose.' The natural man might
think it strange, but the language of the curse was not to
be mistaken. Cursed is every one who has failed to fulfil
the whole law. There was not a person in the whole
world who had not himself sinned in early life. All had
sinned in Adam also, and St. Paul had said in consequence,
'There is none that doeth good, no, not one ! The law
was given not that we might be saved by obeying it, but
that we might know the holiness of God and our own
vileness, and that we might understand that we should
not be damned for nothing. God would have no quarrel-
ling at His just condemning of us at that day.'

This is Bunyan's notion of the position in which we
all naturally stand in this world, and from which the
substitution of Christ's perfect fulfilment of the law alone
rescues us. It is calculated, no doubt, to impress on us
a profound horror of moral evil when the penalty attached to it is so fearful. But it is dangerous to introduce into religion metaphysical conceptions of 'law.'
The cord cracks that is strained too tightly ; and it is
only for brief periods of high spiritual tension that a
theology so merciless can sustain itself. No one with a
conscience in him will think of claiming any merit for
himself. But we know also that there are degrees of
demerit, and, theory or no theory, we fall back on the
first verse of the English Liturgy, as containing a more
endurable account of things.

For this reason, among others, Bunyan disliked the
Liturgy. He thought the doctrine of it false, and he

objected to a Liturgy on principle. He has a sermon on
Prayer, in which he insists that to be worth anything
prayer must be the expression of an inward feeling; and
that people cannot feel in lines laid down for them. Forms
of prayer he thought especially mischievous to children,
as accustoming them to use words to which they attached
no meaning.

'My judgment,' he says, 'is that men go the wrong
way to learn their children to pray. It seems to me a
better way for people to tell their children betimes what
cursed creatures they are, how they are under the wrath
of God by reason of original and actual sin; also to tell
them the nature of God's wrath and the duration of
misery, which if they would conscientiously do, they
would sooner learn their children to pray than they do.
The way that men learn to pray is by conviction of sin,
and this is the way to make our "sweet babes" do so
too.'

'Sweet babes' is unworthy of Bunyan. There is
little sweetness in a state of things so stern as he con-
ceives. He might have considered, too, that there was
a danger of making children unreal in another and worse
sense by teaching them doctrines which neither child nor
man can comprehend. It may be true that a single sin
may consign me to everlasting hell, but I cannot be made
to acknowledge the justice of it. 'Wrath of God' and
such expressions are out of place when we are brought
into the presence of metaphysical laws. Wrath cor-
responds to free-will misused. It is senseless and extravagant when pronounced against actions which men
cannot help, when the faulty action is the necessary consequence of their nature, and the penalty the necessary
consequence of the action.

The same confusion of thought lies in the treatment
of the kindred subjects of Free-will, Election, and Reprobation. The logic must be maintained, and God's
moral attributes simultaneously vindicated. Bunyan
argues about it as ingeniously as Leibnitz himself. Those
who suppose that specific guilt attaches to particular acts,
that all men are put into the world, free to keep the Commandments or to break them, that they are equally able
to do one as to do the other, and are, therefore, proper objects of punishment, hold an opinion which is consistent
in itself, but is in entire contradiction with facts. Children are not as able to control their inclinations as grown
men, and one man is not as able to control himself as
another. Some have no difficulty from the first, and are
constitutionally good ; some are constitutionally weak, or
have incurable propensities for evil. Some are brought
up with care and insight ; others seem never to have any
chance at all. So evident is this, that impartial thinkers
have questioned the reality of human guilt in the sense
in which it is generally understood. Even Butler allows
that if we look too curiously we may have a difficulty in
finding where it lies. And here, if anywhere, there is a
real natural truth in the doctrine of Election, independent
of the merit of those who are so happy as to find favour.
Bunyan, however, reverses the inference. He will have
all guilty together, those who do well and those who do
ill. Even the elect are in themselves as badly off as the
reprobate, and are equally included under sin. Those
who are saved are saved for Christ's merits and not for
their own.

Men of calmer temperament accept facts as they
find them. They are too conscious of their ignorance to
insist on explaining problems which are beyond their

reach. Bunyan lived in an age of intense religious excitement, when the strongest minds were exercising themselves on those questions. It is noticeable that the most
effective intellects inclined to necessitarian conclusions :
some in the shape of Calvinism, some in the correspond-
ing philosophic form of Spinozism. From both alike
there came an absolute submission to the decrees of God,
and a passionate devotion to his service ; while the
morality of Free-will is cold and calculating. Appeals to
a sense of duty do not reach beyond the understanding.
The enthusiasm which will stir men's hearts and give
them a real power of resisting temptation must be
nourished on more invigorating food.

But I need dwell no more on a subject which is un-
suited for these pages.

The object of Bunyan, like that of Luther, like that
of all great spiritual teachers, was to bring his wandering
fellow-mortals into obedience to the commandments, even
while he insisted on the worthlessness of it. He sounded
the strings to others which had sounded loudest in himself. When he passed from mysticism into matters of
ordinary life, he showed the same practical good sense
which distinguishes the chief of all this order of thinkers—
St. Paul. There is a sermon of Bunyan's on Christian behaviour, on the duties of parents to children, and masters to
servants, which might be studied with as much advantage
in English households as the ' Pilgrim's Progress ' itself.
To fathers he says, ' Take heed that the misdeeds for
which thou correctest thy children be not learned them
by thee. Many children learn that wickedness of their
parents, for which they beat and chastise them. Take
heed that thou smile not upon them to encourage them
in small faults, lest that thy carriage to them be an en-

couragement to them to commit greater faults. Take heed that thou use not unsavoury and unseemly words in thy chastising of them, as railing, miscalling, and the like—this is devilish. Take heed that thou do not use them to many chiding words and threatenings, mixed with lightness and laughter. This will harden.'

And again: 'I tell you that if parents carry it lovingly towards their children, mixing their mercies with loving rebukes, and their loving rebukes with fatherly and motherly compassions, they are more likely to save their children than by being churlish and severe to them. Even if these things do not save them, if their mercy do them no good, yet it will greatly ease them at the day of death to consider, I have done by love as much as I could to save and deliver my child from hell.'

Whole volumes on education have said less, or less to the purpose, than these simple words. Unfortunately, parents do not read Bunyan. He is left to children.

Similarly, he says to masters :—

'It is thy duty so to behave thyself to thy servant that thy service may not only be for thy good, but for the good of thy servant, and that in body and soul. Deal with him as to admonition as with thy children. Take heed thou do not turn thy servants into slaves by over-charging them in thy work with thy greediness. Take heed thou carry not thyself to thy servant as he of whom it is said, "He is such a man of Belial that his servants cannot speak to him." The Apostle bids you forbear to threaten them, because you also have a Master in Heaven. Masters, give your servants that which is just, just labour and just wages. Servants that are truly godly care not how cheap they serve their masters, provided they may get into godly families, or where they may be

convenient for the Word.   But if a master or mistress
takes this opportunity to make a prey of their servants,
it is abominable.   I have heard poor servants say that in
some carnal families they have had more liberty to God's
things and more fairness of dealing than among many
professors.   Such masters make religion to stink before
the inhabitants of the land.'

Bunyan was generally charitable in his judgment upon
others.   If there was any exception, it was of Professors
who discredited their calling by conceit and worldliness.

'No sin,' he says, 'reigneth more in the world than
pride among Professors.   The thing is too apparent for
any man to deny.   We may and do see pride display itself in the apparel and carriage of Professors almost as
much as among any in the land.   I have seen church
members so decked and bedaubed with their fangles and
toys that when they have been at worship I have won-
dered with what faces such painted persons could sit in
the place where they were without swooning.   I once
talked with a maid, by way of reproof for her fond and
gaudy garment; she told me the tailor would make it
so.   Poor proud girl, she gave orders to the tailor to make
it so.'

I will give one more extract from Bunyan's pastoral
addresses.   It belongs to a later period in his ministry,
when the law had, for a time, remade Dissent into a crime;
but it will throw light on the part of his story which we
are now approaching, and it is in every way very characteristic of him.   He is speaking to sufferers under persecution.   He says to them :—

' Take heed of being offended with magistrates, because
by their statutes they may cross thy inclinations.   It is
given to them to bear the sword, and a command is to

thee, if thy heart cannot acquiesce with all things, with meekness and patience to suffer. Discontent in the mind sometimes puts discontent into the mouth; and discontent in the mouth doth sometimes also put a halter about thy neck. For as a man speaking a word in jest may for that be hanged in earnest, so he that speaks in discontent may die for it in sober sadness. Above all, get thy conscience possessed more and more with this, that the magistrate is God's ordinance, and is ordered of God as such; that he is the minister of God to thee for good, and that it is thy duty to fear him and to pray for him; to give thanks to God for him and be subject to him; as both Paul and Peter admonish us; and that not only for wrath, but for conscience sake. For all other arguments come short of binding the soul when this argument is wanting, until we believe that of God we are bound thereto.

'I speak not these things as knowing any that are disaffected to the government, for I love to be alone, if not with godly men, in things that are convenient. I speak to show my loyalty to the king, and my love to my fellow-subjects, and my desire that all Christians shall walk in ways of peace and truth.'

CHAPTER V.

ARREST AND TRIAL.

BUNYAN'S preaching enterprise became an extraordinary success. All the Midland Counties heard of his fame, and demanded to hear him. He had been Deacon under Gifford at the Bedford Church; but he was in such request as a preacher, that, in 1657, he was released from his duties there as unable to attend to them. Sects were springing up all over England as weeds in a hotbed. He was soon in controversy; Controversy with Church of England people; Controversy with the Ranters, who believed Christ to be a myth; Controversy with the Quakers who, at their outset, disbelieved in his Divinity and in the inspiration of the Scriptures. Envy at his rapidly acquired reputation brought him baser enemies. He was called a witch, a Jesuit, a highwayman. It was reported that he had 'his misses,' that he had two wives, &c. 'My foes have missed their mark in this,' he said with honest warmth: 'I am not the man. If all the fornicators and adulterers in England were hanged by the neck, John Bunyan, the object of their envy, would be still alive and well. I know not whether there be such a thing as a woman breathing under the cope of the whole heavens but by their apparel, their children, or common fame, except my wife.'

F

But a more serious trial was now before him. Cromwell passed away. The Protectorate came to an end. England decided that it had had enough of Puritans and republicans, and would give the Stuarts and the Established Church another trial. A necessary consequence was the revival of the Act of Uniformity. The Independents were not meek like the Baptists, using no weapons to oppose what they disapproved but passive resistance. The same motives which had determined the original constitution of a Church combining the characters of Protestant and Catholic, instead of leaving religion free, were even more powerful at the Restoration than they had been at the accession of Elizabeth. Before toleration is possible, men must have learnt to tolerate toleration itself; and in times of violent convictions, toleration is looked on as indifference, and indifference as Atheism in disguise. Catholics and Protestants, Churchmen and Dissenters, regarded one another as enemies of God and the State, with whom no peace was possible. Toleration had been tried by the Valois princes in France. Church and chapel had been the rendezvous of armed fanatics. The preachers blew the war-trumpet, and every town and village had been the scene of furious conflicts, which culminated in the Massacre of St. Bartholomew. The same result would have followed in England if the same experiment had been ventured. The different communities were forbidden to have their separate places of worship, and services were contrived which moderate men of all sorts could use and interpret after their own convictions. The instrument required to be delicately handled. It succeeded tolerably as long as Elizabeth lived. When Elizabeth died, the balance was no longer fairly kept. The High Church party obtained the ascendancy and abused

their power.　Tyranny brought revolution, and the
Catholic element in turn disappeared.　The Bishops were
displaced by Presbyterian elders.　The Presbyterian
elders became in turn 'hireling wolves,' 'old priest'
written in new characters.　Cromwell had left conscience
free to Protestants.　But even he had refused equal liberty
to Catholics and Episcopalians.　He was gone too, and
Church and King were back again.　How were they to
stand?　The stern resolute men, to whom the Commonwealth had been the establishment of God's kingdom
upon earth, were as little inclined to keep terms with
Antichrist as the Church people had been inclined to
keep terms with Cromwell.　To have allowed them to
meet openly in their conventicles would have been to
make over the whole of England to them as a seed-bed in
which to plant sedition.　It was pardonable, it was even
necessary, for Charles II. and his advisers to fall back
upon Elizabeth's principles, at least as long as the ashes were
still glowing.　Indulgence had to be postponed till cooler
times.　With the Fifth Monarchy men abroad, every
chapel, except those of the Baptists, would have been a
magazine of explosives.

Under the 35th of Elizabeth, Nonconformists refusing
to attend worship in the parish churches were to be imprisoned till they made their submission.　Three months
were allowed them to consider.　If at the end of that
time they were still obstinate, they were to be banished
the realm ; and if they subsequently returned to England
without permission from the Crown, they were liable to
execution as felons.　This Act had fallen with the Long
Parliament, but at the Restoration it was held to have
revived and to be still in force.　The parish churches
were cleared of their unordained ministers.　The Dis-

senters' chapels were closed. The people were required
by proclamation to be present on Sundays in their proper
place. So the majority of the nation had decided. If
they had wished for religious liberty they would not have
restored the Stuarts, or they would have insisted on conditions, and would have seen that they were observed.

Venner's plot showed the reality of the danger and
justified the precaution.

The Baptists and Quakers might have been trusted
to discourage violence, but it was impossible to distinguish among the various sects, whose tenets were unknown
and even unsettled. The great body of Cromwell's spiritual supporters believed that armed resistance to a government which they disapproved was not only lawful, but
was enjoined.

Thus, no sooner was Charles II. on the throne than
the Nonconformists found themselves again under bondage. Their separate meetings were prohibited, and they
were not only forbidden to worship in their own fashion,
but they had to attend church, under penalties. The
Bedford Baptists refused to obey. Their meeting-house
in the town was shut up, but they continued to assemble
in woods and outhouses ; Bunyan preaching to them as
before, and going to the place in disguise. Informers
were soon upon his track. The magistrates had received
orders to be vigilant. Bunyan was the most prominent Dissenter in the neighbourhood. He was too sensible to court martyrdom. He had intended to leave
the town till more quiet times, and had arranged to meet
a few of his people once more to give them a parting
address. It was November 12, 1660. The place agreed
on was a house in the village of Samsell near Harling-
ton. Notice of his intention was privately conveyed to

Mr. Wingate, a magistrate in the adjoining district. The constables were set to watch the house, and were directed to bring Bunyan before him. Some member of the congregation heard of it. Bunyan was warned, and was advised to stay at home that night, or else to conceal himself. His departure had been already arranged; but when he learnt that a warrant was actually out against him, he thought that he was bound to stay and face the danger. He was the first Nonconformist who had been marked for arrest. If he flinched after he had been singled out by name, the whole body of his congregation would be discouraged. Go to church he would not, or promise to go to church; but he was willing to suffer whatever punishment the law might order. Thus at the time and place which had been agreed on, he was in the room, at Samsell, with his Bible in his hand, and was about to begin his address, when the constables entered and arrested him. He made no resistance. He desired only to be allowed to say a few words, which the constables permitted. He then prepared to go with them. He was not treated with any roughness. It was too late to take him that night before the magistrate. His friends undertook for his appearance when he should be required, and he went home with them. The constables came for him again on the following afternoon.

Mr. Wingate, when the information was first brought to him, supposed that he had fallen on a nest of Fifth Monarchy men. He enquired, when Bunyan was brought in, how many arms had been found at the meeting. When he learnt that there were no arms, and that it had no political character whatever, he evidently thought it was a matter of no consequence. He told Bunyan that he had been breaking the law, and asked him why he could

not attend to his business.   Bunyan said that his object
in teaching was merely to persuade people to give up their
sins.   He could do that and attend to his business also.
Wingate answered that the law must be obeyed.   He
must commit Bunyan for trial at the Quarter Sessions ; but
he would take bail for him, if his securities would engage
that he would not preach again meanwhile.   Bunyan refused to be bailed on any such terms.   Preach he would
and must, and the recognizances would be forfeited.   After
such an answer, Wingate could only send him to gaol :
he could not help himself.   The committal was made out,
and Bunyan was being taken away, when two of his
friends met him, who were acquainted with Wingate, and
they begged the constable to wait.   They went in to the
magistrate.   They told him who and what Bunyan was.
The magistrate had not the least desire to be hard, and it
was agreed that if he would himself give some general
promise of a vague kind he might be let go altogether.
Bunyan was called back.   Another magistrate who knew
him had by this time joined Wingate.   They both said
that they were reluctant to send him to prison.   If he
would promise them that he would not call the people together any more, he might go home.

They had purposely chosen a form of words which
would mean as little as possible.   But Bunyan would not
accept an evasion.   He said that he would not force the
people to come together, but if he was in a place where
the people were met, he should certainly speak to them.
The magistrate repeated that the meetings were unlawful.
They would be satisfied if Bunyan would simply promise
that he would not call such meetings.   It was as plain as
possible that they wished to dismiss the case, and they
were thrusting words into his mouth which he could use

without a mental reservation; but he persisted that there were many ways in which a meeting might be called; if people came together to hear him, knowing that he would speak, he might be said to have called them together.

Remonstrances and entreaties were equally useless, and, with extreme unwillingness, they committed him to Bedford Gaol to wait for the sessions.

It is not for us to say that Bunyan was too precise. He was himself the best judge of what his conscience and his situation required. To himself, at any rate, his trial was at the moment most severe. He had been left a widower a year or two before, with four young children, one of them blind. He had lately married a second time. His wife was pregnant. The agitation at her husband's arrest brought on premature labour, and she was lying in his house in great danger. He was an affectionate man, and the separation at such a time was peculiarly distressing. After some weeks the quarter sessions came on. Bunyan was indicted under the usual form, that he ' being a person of such and such condition had since such a time devilishly and perniciously abstained from coming to church to hear Divine service, and was a common upholder of unlawful meetings and conventicles, to the great disturbance and distraction of the good subjects of this kingdom, contrary to the laws of our Sovereign Lord the King.'

There seems to have been a wish to avoid giving him a formal trial. He was not required to plead, and it may have been thought that he had been punished sufficiently. He was asked why he did not go to church? He said that the Prayer-book was made by man; he was ordered in the Bible to pray with the spirit and the understanding, not with the spirit and the Prayer-book. The magistrates, referring to another Act of Parliament, cautioned Bunyan against finding fault with the Prayer-book, or he would bring himself into further trouble.   Justice Keelin who presided said (so Bunyan declares, and it has been the standing jest of his biographers ever since) that the Prayer-book had been in use ever since the Apostles' time.   Perhaps the words were that parts of it had been then in use (the Apostles' Creed, for instance), and thus they would have been strictly true.   However this might be, they told him kindly, as Mr. Wingate had done, that it would be better for him if he would keep to his proper work.   The law had prohibited conventicles.   He might teach, if he pleased, in his own family and among his friends.   He must not call large numbers of people together.   He was as impracticable as before, and the magistrates, being but unregenerate mortals, may be pardoned if they found him provoking.   If, he said, it was lawful for him to do good to a few, it must be equally lawful to do good to many.   He had a gift, which he was bound to use.   If it was sinful for men to meet together to exhort one another to follow Christ, he should sin still.

He was compelling the Court to punish him, whether they wished it or not.   He describes the scene as if the choice had rested with the magistrates to convict him or to let him go.   If he was bound to do his duty, they were equally bound to do theirs.   They took his answers as a plea of guilty to the indictment, and Justice Keelin, who was chairman, pronounced his sentence in the terms of the Act.   He was to go to prison for three months; if, at the end of three months, he still refused to conform, he was to be transported ; and if he came back without license he would be hanged.   Bunyan merely answered, ' If I

were out of prison to-day, I would preach the Gospel again
to-morrow.'   More might have followed, but the gaoler
led him away.

There were three gaols in Bedford, and no evidence
has been found to show in which of the three Bunyan was
confined.   Two of them, the county gaol and the town
gaol, were large roomy buildings.   Tradition has chosen
the third, a small lock-up, fourteen feet square, which
stood over the river between the central arches of the
old bridge ; and as it appears from the story that he had
at times fifty or sixty fellow-prisoners, and as he admits
himself that he was treated at first with exceptional
kindness, it may be inferred that tradition, in selecting
the prison on the bridge, was merely desiring to exhibit
the sufferings of the Nonconformist martyr in a sensational form, and that he was never in this prison at all.
When it was pulled down in 1811 a gold ring was found
in the rubbish, with the initials 'J. B.' upon it.   This
is one of the 'trifles light as air' which carry conviction to the 'jealous' only, and is too slight a foundation
on which to assert a fact so inherently improbable.

When the three months were over, the course of law
would have brought him again to the bar, when he
would have had to choose between conformity and exile.
There was still the same desire to avoid extremities, and
as the day approached, the clerk of the peace was sent
to persuade him into some kind of compliance. Various
insurrections had broken out since his arrest, and must
have shown him, if he could have reflected, that there
was real reason for the temporary enforcement of the
Act.   He was not asked to give up preaching.   He was
asked only to give up public preaching.   It was well
known that he had no disposition to rebellion.   Even the

going to church was not insisted on. The clerk of the
peace told him that he might 'exhort his neighbours in
private discourse,' if only he would not bring the people
together in numbers, which the magistrates would be
bound to notice. In this way he might continue his use-
fulness, and would not be interfered with.

Bunyan knew his own freedom from seditious intentions. He would not see that the magistrates could not
suspend the law and make an exception in his favour.
They were going already to the utmost limit of indulgence.
But the more he disapproved of rebellion, the more punc-
tilious he was in carrying out resistance of another kind
which he held to be legitimate. He was a representative
person, and he thought that in yielding he would hurt
the cause of religious liberty. 'The law,' he said, 'had
provided two ways of obeying—one to obey actively, and
if he could not in conscience obey actively, then to suffer
whatever penalty was inflicted on him.'

The clerk of the peace could produce no effect. Bunyan rather looked on him as a false friend trying to
entangle him. The three months elapsed, and the magistrates had to determine what was to be done. If Bunyan
was brought before them, they must exile him. His case
was passed over and he was left in prison, where his wife
and children were allowed to visit him daily. He did not
understand the law or appreciate their forbearance. He
exaggerated his danger. At the worst he could only have
been sent to America, where he might have remained as
long as he pleased. He feared that he might perhaps be
hanged.

'I saw what was coming,' he said, 'and had two
considerations especially on my heart, how to be able to
endure, should my imprisonment be long and tedious, and

how to be able to encounter death should that be my portion. I was made to see that if I would suffer rightly, I must pass sentence of death upon everything that can properly be called a thing of this life, even to reckon myself, my wife, my children, my health, my enjoyments all as dead to me, and myself as dead to them. Yet I was a man compassed with infirmities. The parting with my wife and poor children hath often been to me in this place (the prison in which he was writing) as the pulling of my flesh from my bones ; and that not only because I am too, too, fond of those great mercies, but also because I should have often brought to my mind the hardships, miseries, and wants my poor family was like to meet with should I be taken from them, especially my poor blind child, who lay nearer my heart than all I had besides. Poor child, thought I, what sorrow art thou like to have for thy portion in this world ! Thou must be beaten, suffer hunger, cold, nakedness, and a thousand calamities, though I cannot now endure the wind should blow on thee. But yet, thought I, I must venture all with God, though it goeth to the quick to leave you. I was as a man who was pulling down his house upon the head of his wife and children. Yet thought I, I must do it—I must do it. I had this for consideration, that if I should now venture all for God, I engaged God to take care of my concernments. Also I had dread of the torments of hell, which I was sure they must partake of that for fear of the cross do shrink from their profession. I had this much upon my spirit, that my imprisonment might end in the gallows for aught I could tell. In the condition I now was in I was not fit to die, nor indeed did I think I could if I should be called to it. I feared I might show a weak heart, and give occasion to the enemy. This lay with

great trouble on me, for methought I was ashamed to die
with a pale face and tottering knees for such a cause as
this.   The things of God were kept out of my sight.
The tempter followed me with, "But whither must you
go when you die?   What will become of you?   What
evidence have you for heaven and glory, and an inheritance among them that are sanctified?"   Thus was I
tossed many weeks; but I felt it was for the Word and
way of God that I was in this condition.   God might
give me comfort or not as He pleased.   I was bound, but
He was free—yea, it was my duty to stand to His Word,
whether He would ever look upon me or no, or save me
at the last.   Wherefore, thought I, the point being thus,
I am for going on and venturing my eternal state with
Christ, whether I have comfort here or no.   If God does
not come in, thought I, I will leap off the ladder even
blindfold into eternity, sink or swim, come heaven, come
hell.   Now was my heart full of comfort.'

The ladder was an imaginary ladder, but the resolu-
tion was a genuine manly one, such as lies at the bottom
of all brave and honourable action.   Others who have
thought very differently from Bunyan about such matters
have felt the same as he felt.   Be true to yourself whatever comes, even if damnation come.   Better hell with an
honest heart, than heaven with cowardice and insincerity.
It was the more creditable to Bunyan, too, because the
spectres and hobgoblins had begun occasionally to revisit
him.

'Of all temptations I ever met with in my life,' he
says, 'to question the being of God and the truth of His
Gospel is the worst and worst to be borne.   When this
temptation comes it takes my girdle from me and removes
the foundation from under me.   Though God has visited

my soul with never so blessed a discovery of Himself, yet afterwards I have been in my spirit so filled with darkness, that I could not so much as once conceive what that God and that comfort was with which I had been refreshed.'

CHAPTER VI.

THE BEDFORD GAOL.

THE irregularities in the proceedings against Bunyan had perhaps been suggested by the anticipation of the general pardon which was expected in the following spring. At the coronation of Charles, April 23, 1661, an order was issued for the release of prisoners who were in gaol for any offences short of felony. Those who were waiting their trials were to be let go at once. Those convicted and under sentence might sue out a pardon under the Great Seal at any time within a year from the proclamation. Was Bunyan legally convicted or not ? He had not pleaded directly to the indictment. No evidence had been heard against him. His trial had been a conversation between himself and the Court. The point had been raised by his friends. His wife had been in London to make interest for him, and a peer had presented a petition in Bunyan's behalf in the House of Lords. The judges had been directed to look again into the matter at the midsummer assizes. The high sheriff was active in Bunyan's favour. The Judges Twisden, Chester, and no less a person than Sir Matthew Hale, appear to have concluded that his conviction was legal, that he could not be tried again, and that he must apply for pardon in the regular way. His wife, however, at the instance of the

sheriff, obtained a hearing, and they listened courteously
to what she had to say. When she had done, Mr. Justice
Twisden put the natural question, whether, if her husband was released, he would refrain from preaching in
public for the future. If he intended to repeat his offence
immediately that he was at liberty, his liberty would only
bring him into a worse position. The wife at once said
that he dared not leave off preaching as long as he could
speak. The judge asked if she thought her husband was
to be allowed to do as he pleased. She said that he was
a peaceable person, and wished only to be restored to a
position in which he could maintain his family. They
had four small children who could not help themselves,
one of them being blind, and they had nothing to live
upon as long as her husband was in prison but the charity
of their friends. Hale remarked that she looked very
young to have four children. 'I am but mother-in-law
to them,' she said, 'having not been married yet full two
years. I was with child when my husband was first apprehended, but being young, I being dismayed at the
news fell in labour, and so continued for eight days. I
was delivered, but my child died.'

Hale was markedly kind. He told her that as the
conviction had been recorded they could not set it aside.
She might sue out a pardon if she pleased, or she might
obtain 'a writ of error,' which would be simpler and less
expensive.

She left the court in tears—tears, however, which
were not altogether tears of suffering innocence. 'It was
not so much,' she said, 'because they were so hardhearted
against me and my husband, but to think what a sad account such poor creatures would have to give at the
coming of the Lord.' No doubt both Bunyan and she

thought themselves cruelly injured, and they confounded
the law with the administration of it. Persons better informed than they often choose to forget that judges are
sworn to administer the law which they find, and rail at
them as if the sentences which they are obliged by their
oaths to pass were their own personal acts.

A pardon, it cannot be too often said, would have been
of no use to Bunyan, because he was determined to persevere in disobeying a law which he considered to be un-
just. The most real kindness which could be shown to
him was to leave him where he was. His imprisonment
was intended to be little more than nominal. His gaoler,
not certainly without the sanction of the sheriff, let him
go where he pleased; once even so far as London. He
used his liberty as he had declared that he would. ' I followed my wonted course of preaching,' he says, ' taking
all occasions that were put in my hand to visit the people
of God.' This was deliberate defiance. The authorities
saw that he must be either punished in earnest or the
law would fall into contempt. He admitted that he expected to be ' roundly dealt with.' His indulgences were
withdrawn, and he was put into close confinement.

Sessions now followed sessions, and assizes, assizes.
His detention was doubtless irregular, for by law he
should have been sent beyond the seas. He petitioned
to be brought to trial again, and complained loudly that
his petition was not listened to ; but no legislator, in
framing an Act of Parliament, ever contemplated an
offender in so singular a position. Bunyan was simply
trying his strength against the Crown and Parliament.
The judges and magistrates respected his character, and
were unwilling to drive him out of the country ; he had
himself no wish for liberty on that condition. The only

resource, therefore, was to prevent him forcibly from re-peating an offence that would compel them to adopt harsh measures which they were so earnestly trying to avoid.

Such was the world-famous imprisonment of John Bunyan, which has been the subject of so much eloquent declamation. It lasted in all for more than twelve years. It might have ended at any time if he would have pro-mised to confine his addresses to a private circle. It did end after six years. He was released under the first de-claration of indulgence; but as he instantly recommenced his preaching, he was arrested again. Another six years went by; he was again let go, and was taken once more immediately after, preaching in a wood. This time he was detained but a few months, and in form more than reality. The policy of the government was then changed, and he was free for the rest of his life.

His condition during his long confinement has fur-nished a subject for pictures which if correct would be extremely affecting. It is true that, being unable to attend to his usual business, he spent his unoccupied hours in making tags for bootlaces. With this one fact to build on, and with the assumption that the scene of his sufferings was the Bridge Lockhouse, Nonconformist imagination has drawn a ' den ' for us, ' where there was not a yard or a court to walk in for daily exercise;' 'a damp and dreary cell;' 'a narrow chink which admits a few scanty rays of light to render visible the abode of woe;' 'the prisoner, pale and emaciated, seated on the humid earth, pursuing his daily task, to earn the morsel which prolongs his existence and his confinement together. Near him, reclining in pensive sadness, his blind daughter, five other distressed children, and an affectionate wife, whom pinching want and grief have worn down to the gate of death. Ten summer suns have rolled over the mansion of his misery whose reviving rays have never once penetrated his sad abode,' &c. &c.

If this description resembles or approaches the truth, I can but say that to have thus abandoned to want their most distinguished pastor and his family was intensely discreditable to the Baptist community. English prisons in the seventeenth century were not models of good management. But prisoners, whose friends could pay for them, were not consigned to damp and dreary cells; and in default of evidence of which not a particle exists, I cannot charge so reputable a community with a neglect so scandalous. The entire story is in itself incredible. Bunyan was prosperous in his business. He was respected and looked up to by a large and growing body of citizens, including persons of wealth and position in London. He was a representative sufferer fighting the battle of all the Nonconformists in England. He had active supporters in the town of Bedford and among the gentlemen of the county. The authorities, so far as can be inferred from their actions, tried from the first to deal as gently with him as he would allow them to do. Is it conceivable that the Baptists would have left his family to starve; or that his own confinement would have been made so absurdly and needlessly cruel? Is it not far more likely that he found all the indulgences which money could buy and the rules of the prison would allow? Bunyan is not himself responsible for these wild legends. Their real character appears more clearly when we observe how he was occupied during these years.

Friends, in the first place, had free access to him, and strangers who were drawn to him by reputation; while the gaol was considered a private place, and he was allowed to preach there, at least occasionally, to his fellow-prisoners. Charles Doe, a distinguished Nonconformist, visited him in his confinement, and has left an account of what he saw. 'When I was there,' he writes, 'there were about sixty dissenters besides himself, taken but a little before at a religious meeting at Kaistor, in the county of Bedford, besides two eminent dissenting ministers, Mr. Wheeler and Mr. Dun, by which means the prison was much crowded. Yet, in the midst of all that hurry, I heard Mr. Bunyan both preach and pray with that mighty spirit of faith and plerophory of Divine assistance, that he made me stand and wonder. Here they could sing without fear of being overheard, no informers prowling round, and the world shut out.'

This was not all. A fresh and more severe Conventicle Act was passed in 1670. Attempts were made to levy fines in the town of Bedford. There was a riot there. The local officers refused to assist in quelling it. The shops were shut. Bedford was occupied by soldiers. Yet, at this very time, Bunyan was again allowed to go abroad through general connivance. He spent his nights with his family. He even preached now and then in the woods. Once when he had intended to be out for the night, information was given to a clerical magistrate in the neighbourhood, who disliked him, and a constable was sent to ascertain if the prisoners were all within ward. Bunyan had received a hint of what was coming. He was in his place when the constable came; and the governor of the gaol is reported to have said to him, 'You may go out when you please, for you know better when to return than I can tell you.' Parliament might pass laws, but the execution of them depended on the local

authorities. Before the Declaration of Indulgence, the
Baptist church in Bedford was reopened. Bunyan, while
still nominally in confinement, attended its meetings. In
1671 he became an Elder; in December of that year he
was chosen Pastor. The question was raised whether, as
a prisoner, he was eligible. The objection would not have
been set aside had he been unable to undertake the duties
of the office. These facts prove conclusively that, for a
part at least of the twelve years, the imprisonment was
little more than formal. He could not have been in the
Bridge Gaol when he had sixty fellow-prisoners, and
was able to preach to them in private. It is unlikely
that at any time he was made to suffer any greater hardships than were absolutely inevitable.

But whether Bunyan's confinement was severe or easy,
it was otherwise of inestimable value to him. It gave
him leisure to read and reflect. Though he preached
often, yet there must have been intervals, perhaps long
intervals, of compulsory silence. The excitement of perpetual speech-making is fatal to the exercise of the higher
qualities. The periods of calm enabled him to discover
powers in himself of which he might otherwise have
never known the existence. Of books he had but few;
for a time only the Bible and Foxe's 'Martyrs.' But the
Bible thoroughly known is a literature of itself—the
rarest and the richest in all departments of thought or
imagination which exists. Foxe's 'Martyrs,' if he had
a complete edition of it, would have given him a very
adequate knowledge of history. With those two books
he had no cause to complain of intellectual destitution.
He must have read more, however. He knew George
Herbert—perhaps Spenser—perhaps 'Paradise Lost.'
But of books, except of the Bible, he was at no time a

great student. Happily for himself, he had no other book
of Divinity, and he needed none. His real study was
human life as he had seen it, and the human heart as he
had experienced the workings of it. Though he never
mastered successfully the art of verse, he had other gifts
which belong to a true poet. He had imagination, if
not of the highest, yet of a very high order. He had
infinite inventive humour, tenderness, and, better than
all, powerful masculine sense. To obtain the use of these
faculties he needed only composure, and this his imprisonment secured for him. He had published several theological compositions before his arrest, which have re-
latively little value. Those which he wrote in prison—
even on theological subjects—would alone have made
him a reputation as a Nonconformist divine. In no
other writings are the peculiar views of Evangelical Calvinism brought out more clearly, or with a more heart-
felt conviction of their truth. They have furnished an
arsenal from which English Protestant divines have ever
since equipped themselves. The most beautiful of them,
' Grace Abounding to the Chief of Sinners,' is his own
spiritual biography, which contains the account of his
early history. The first part of the ' Pilgrim's Progress '
was composed there as an amusement. To this, and to
his other works which belong to literature, I shall return
in a future chapter.

Visitors who saw him in the gaol found his manner
and presence as impressive as his writings. ' He was
mild and affable in conversation,' says one of them, ' not
given to loquacity or to much discourse, unless some
urgent occasion required. It was observed he never spoke
of himself or of his talents, but seemed low in his own
eyes. He was never heard to reproach or revile any,

whatever injury he received, but rather rebuked those who did so. He managed all things with such exactness as if he had made it his study not to give offence.'

The final 'Declaration of Indulgence' came at last, bringing with it the privilege for which Bunyan had fought and suffered. Charles II. cared as little for liberty as his father or his brother, but he wished to set free the Catholics, and as a step towards it he conceded a general toleration to the Protestant Dissenters. Within two years of the passing of the Conventicle Act of 1670, this and every other penal law against Nonconformists was suspended. They were allowed to open their 'meeting houses' for 'worship and devotion,' subject only to a few easy conditions. The localities were to be specified in which chapels were required, and the ministers were to receive their licenses from the Crown. To prevent suspicions, the Roman Catholics were for the present excluded from the benefit of the concession. Mass could be said, as before, only in private houses. A year later the Proclamation was confirmed by Act of Parliament.

Thus Bunyan's long imprisonment was ended. The cause was won. He had been its foremost representative and champion, and was one of the first persons to receive the benefit of the change of policy. He was now forty-four years old. The order for his release was signed on May 8, 1672. His license as pastor of the Baptist chapel at Bedford was issued on the 9th. He established himself in a small house in the town. 'When he came abroad,' says one, 'he found his temporal affairs were gone to wreck, and he had as to them to begin again as if he had newly come into the world. But yet he was not destitute of friends who had all along supported him with necessaries, and had been very good to his family: so that by

their assistance, getting things a little about him again,
he resolved, as much as possible, to decline worldly business, and give himself wholly up to the service of God.'
As much as possible; but not entirely. In 1685, being
afraid of a return of persecution, he made over, as a precaution, his whole estate to his wife; 'All and singular
his goods, chattels, debts, ready money, plate, rings,
household stuff, apparel, utensils, brass, pewter, bedding,
and all his other substance.' In this deed he still describes himself as a brazier. The language is that of a
man in easy, if not ample circumstances. 'Though by
reason of losses which he sustained by imprisonment,'
says another biographer, 'his treasures swelled not to
excess, he always had sufficient to live decently and
creditably.' His writings and his sufferings had made
him famous throughout England. He became the actual
head of the Baptist community. Men called him, half in
irony, half in seriousness, Bishop Bunyan, and he passed
the rest of his life honourably and innocently, occupied
in writing, preaching, district visiting, and opening
daughter churches. Happy in his work, happy in the
sense that his influence was daily extending—spreading
over his own country, and to the far-off settlements in
America, he spent his last years in his own land of
Beulah, Doubting Castle out of sight, and the towers and
minarets of Emmanuel Land growing nearer and clearer
as the days went on.

He had not detected, or at least, at first, he did not
detect, the sinister purpose which lay behind the Indulgence. The exception of the Roman Catholics gave him
perfect confidence in the Government, and after his release
he published a 'Discourse upon Antichrist,' with a pre-
face, in which he credited Charles with the most righteous

intentions, and urged his countrymen to be loyal and
faithful to him. His object in writing it, he said, ' was
to testify his loyalty to the King, his love to the brethren,
and his service to his country.' Antichrist was of course
the Pope, the deadliest of all enemies to vital Christianity.
To its kings and princes England owed its past deliverance from him. To kings England must look for his final
overthrow.

' As the noble King Henry VIII. did cast down the
Antichristian worship, so he cast down the laws that
held it up; so also did the good King Edward his son.
The brave Queen Elizabeth, also, the sister of King Edward, left of things of this nature to her lasting fame
behind her.' Cromwell he dared not mention—perhaps
he did not wish to mention him. But he evidently believed that there was better hope in Charles Stuart than
in conspiracy and revolution.

' Kings,' he said, ' must be the men that shall down
with Antichrist, and they shall down with her in God's
time. God hath begun to draw the hearts of some of
them from her already, and He will set them in time
against her round about. If, therefore, they do not that
work so fast as we would have them, let us exercise
patience and hope in God. 'Tis a wonder they go as fast
as they do since the concerns of whole kingdoms lie upon
their shoulders, and there are so many Sanballats and
Tobias's to flatter them and misinform them. Let the
King have visibly a place in your hearts, and with heart
and mouth give God thanks for him. He is a better
Saviour of us than we may be aware of, and hath delivered us from more deaths than we can tell how to
think. We are bidden to give God thanks for all men,
and in the first place for kings, and all that are in autho-

rity. Be not angry with them, no not in thy thought.
But consider if they go not in the work of Reformation
so fast as thou wouldest they should, the fault may be
thine. Know that thou also hast thy cold and chill
frames of heart, and sittest still when thou shouldest be
up and doing. Pray for the long life of the King. Pray
that God would give wisdom and judgment to the King.
Pray that God would discern all plots and conspiracies
against his person and government. I do confess myself
one of the old-fashioned professors that wish to fear God
and honour the King. I am also for blessing them that
curse me, for doing good to them that hate me, and for
praying for them that despitefully use me and persecute
me ; and I have had more peace in the practice of these
things than all the world are aware of.'

The Stuarts, both Charles and James, were grateful
for Bunyan's services. The Nonconformists generally
went up and down in Royal favour ; lost their privileges
and regained them as their help was needed or could be
dispensed with. But Bunyan was never more molested.
He did what he liked. He preached where he pleased,
and no one troubled him or called him to account. He
was not insincere. His constancy in enduring so long an
imprisonment which a word from him would have ended,
lifts him beyond the reach of unworthy suspicions. But
he disapproved always of violent measures. His rule
was to submit to the law ; and where, as he said, he
could not obey actively, then to bear with patience the
punishment that might be inflicted on him. Perhaps he
really hoped, as long as hope was possible, that good
might come out of the Stuarts.

CHAPTER VII.

LIFE AND DEATH OF MR. BADMAN.

To his contemporaries Bunyan was known as the Non-conformist Martyr, and the greatest living Protestant preacher. To us he is mainly interesting through his writings, and especially through the ' Pilgrim's Progress.' Although he possessed, in a remarkable degree, the gift of expressing himself in written words, he had himself no value for literature. He cared simply for spiritual truth, and literature in his eyes was only useful as a means of teaching it. Every thing with which a reasonable man could concern himself was confined within the limits of Christian faith and practice. Ambition was folly. Amusement was idle trifling in a life so short as man's, and with issues so far-reaching depending upon it. To understand, and to make others understand, what Christ had done, and what Christ required men to do, was the occupation of his whole mind, and no object ever held his attention except in connection with it. With a purpose so strict, and a theory of religion so precise, there is usually little play for imagination or feeling. Though we read Protestant theology as a duty, we find it as dry in the mouth as sawdust. The literature which would please must represent nature, and nature refuses to be bound into our dogmatic systems. No object can be pictured truly, except by a mind which has sympathy with it.   Shakespeare no more hates Iago than Iago hates himself. He allows Iago to exhibit himself in his own way, as nature does. Every character, if justice is to be done to it, must be painted at its best, as it appears to itself; and a man impressed deeply with religious convictions is generally incapable of the sympathy which would give him an insight into what he disapproves and dislikes.   And yet Bunyan, intensely religious as he was, and narrow as his theology was, is always human.   His genius remains fresh and vigorous under the least promising conditions. All mankind being under sin together, he has no favourites to flatter, no opponents to misrepresent. There is a kindliness in his descriptions, even of the Evil One's attacks upon himself.

The 'Pilgrim's Progress,' though professedly an allegoric story of the Protestant plan of salvation, is conceived in the large, wide spirit of humanity itself. Anglo-Catholic and Lutheran, Calvinist and Deist can alike read it with delight, and find their own theories in it.   Even the Romanist has only to blot out a few paragraphs, and can discover no purer model of a Christian life to place in the hands of his children.   The religion of the 'Pilgrim's Progress' is the religion which must be always and everywhere, as long as man believes that he has a soul and is responsible for his actions; and thus it is that, while theological folios once devoured as manna from Heaven now lie on the bookshelves dead as Egyptian mummies, this book is wrought into the mind and memory of every well-conditioned English or American child; while the matured man, furnished with all the knowledge which literature can teach him, still finds the adventures of Christian as charming as the adventures of Ulysses or Æneas. He sees there the reflexion of

himself, the familiar features of his own nature, which
remain the same from era to era. Time cannot impair its
interest, or intellectual progress make it cease to be true
to experience.

But the 'Pilgrim's Progress,' though the best known,
is not the only work of imagination which Bunyan produced; he wrote another religious allegory, which Lord
Macaulay thought would have been the best of its kind
in the world if the 'Pilgrim's Progress' had not existed.
The 'Life of Mr. Badman,' though now scarcely read at
all, contains a vivid picture of rough English life in the
days of Charles II. Bunyan was a poet, too, in the technical sense of the word, and though he disclaimed the name,
and though rhyme and metre were to him as Saul's
armour to David, the fine quality of his mind still shows
itself in the uncongenial accoutrements.

It has been the fashion to call Bunyan's verse doggerel; but no verse is doggerel which has a sincere and
rational meaning in it. Goethe, who understood his own
trade, says that the test of poetry is the substance which
remains when the poetry is reduced to prose. Bunyan
had infinite invention. His mind was full of objects
which he had gathered at first hand, from observation
and reflection. He had excellent command of the English
language, and could express what he wished with sharp,
defined outlines, and without the waste of a word. The
rhythmical structure of his prose is carefully correct.
Scarcely a syllable is ever out of place. His ear for verse,
though less true, is seldom wholly at fault, and whether
in prose or verse, he had the superlative merit that he
could never write nonsense. If one of the motives of
poetical form be to clothe thought and feeling in the dress
in which it can be most easily remembered, Bunyan's

lines are often as successful as the best lines of Quarles or George Herbert. Who, for instance, could forget these ?—

> Sin is the worm of hell, the lasting fire :
> Hell would soon lose its heat should sin expire ;
> Better sinless in hell than to be where
> Heaven is, and to be found a sinner there.

Or these, on persons whom the world calls men of spirit :—

> Though you dare crack a coward's crown,
> 　Or quarrel for a pin,
> You dare not on the wicked frown,
> 　Or speak against their sin.

The 'Book of Ruth' and the 'History of Joseph' done into blank verse are really beautiful idylls. The substance with which he worked, indeed, is so good that there would be a difficulty in spoiling it completely ; but the prose of the translation in the English Bible, faultless as it is, loses nothing in Bunyan's hands, and if we found these poems in the collected works of a poet laureate, we should consider that a difficult task had been accomplished successfully. Bunyan felt, like the translators of the preceding century, that the text was sacred, that his duty was to give the exact meaning of it, without epithets or ornaments, and thus the original grace is completely preserved.

Of a wholly different kind, and more after Quarles's manner, is a collection of thoughts in verse, which he calls a book for boys and girls. All his observations ran naturally in one direction ; to minds possessed and governed by religion, nature, be their creed what it may, is always a parable reflecting back their own views.

But how neatly expressed are these 'Meditations upon an Egg':—

> The egg's no chick by falling from a hen,
> Nor man's a Christian till he's born again;
> The egg's at first contained in the shell,
> Men afore grace in sin and darkness dwell;
> The egg, when laid, by warmth is made a chicken,
> And Christ by grace the dead in sin doth quicken;
> The egg when first a chick the shell's its prison,
> So flesh to soul who yet with Christ is risen.

Or this, 'On a Swallow':—

> This pretty bird! Oh, how she flies and sings;
> But could she do so if she had not wings?
> Her wings bespeak my faith, her songs my peace;
> When I believe and sing, my doubtings cease.

Though the Globe Theatre was, in the opinion of Nonconformists, 'the heart of Satan's empire,' Bunyan must yet have known something of Shakespeare. In the second part of the 'Pilgrim's Progress' we find :—

> Who would true valour see,
> Let him come hither;
> One here will constant be,
> Come wind, come weather.

The resemblance to the song in 'As You Like It' is too near to be accidental :—

> Who doth ambition shun,
> And loves to be in the sun;
> Seeking the food he eats,
> And pleased with what he gets,
> Come hither, come hither, come hither.
> Here shall be no enemy,
> Save winter and rough weather.

Bunyan may, perhaps, have heard the lines, and the rhymes may have clung to him without his knowing whence they came. But he would never have been heard of outside his own communion, if his imagination had found no better form of expression for itself than verse. His especial gift was for allegory, the single form of imaginative fiction which he would not have considered trivial, and his especial instrument was plain, unaffected Saxon prose. 'The Holy War' is a people's Paradise Lost and Paradise Regained in one. The 'Life of Mr. Badman' is a didactic tale, describing the career of a vulgar, middle-class, unprincipled scoundrel.

These are properly Bunyan's 'works,' the results of his life so far as it affects the present generation of Englishmen; and as they are little known, I shall give an account of each of them.

The 'Life of Badman' is presented as a dialogue between Mr. Wiseman and Mr. Attentive. Mr. Wiseman tells the story, Mr. Attentive comments upon it. The names recall Bunyan's well-known manner. The figures stand for typical characters; but as the *dramatis personæ* of many writers of fiction, while professing to be beings of flesh and blood are no more than shadows, so Bunyan's shadows are solid men whom we can feel and handle.

Mr. Badman is, of course, one of the 'reprobate.' Bunyan considered theoretically that a reprobate may to outward appearance have the graces of a saint, and that there may be little in his conduct to mark his true character. A reprobate may be sorry for his sins, he may repent and lead a good life. He may reverence good men and may try to resemble them; he may pray, and his prayers may be answered; he may have the spirit of God, and may receive another heart, and yet he may be under the covenant of works, and may be eternally lost. This Bunyan could say while he was writing theology; but art has its rules as well as its more serious sister, and when he had to draw a living specimen, he drew him as he had seen him in his own Bedford neighbourhood.

Badman showed from childhood a propensity for evil, He was so 'addicted to lying that his parents could not distinguish when he was speaking the truth. He would invent, tell, and stand to the lies which he invented, with such an audacious face, that one might read in his very countenance the symptoms of a hard and desperate heart. It was not the fault of his parents; they were much dejected at the beginnings of their son, nor did he want counsel and correction, if that would have made him better : but all availed nothing.'

Lying was not Badman's only fault. He took to pilfering and stealing. He robbed his neighbours' orchards. He picked up money if he found it lying about. Especially, Mr. Wiseman notes that he hated Sundays. ' Reading Scriptures, godly conferences, repeating of sermons and prayers, were things that he could not away with.' ' He was an enemy to that day, because more restraint was laid upon him from his own ways than was possible on any other.' Mr. Wiseman never doubts that the Puritan Sunday ought to have been appreciated by little boys. If a child disliked it, the cause could only be his own wickedness. Young Badman ' was greatly given also to swearing and cursing.' ' He made no more of it ' than Mr. Wiseman made ' of telling his fingers.' ' He counted it a glory to swear and curse, and it was as natural to him as to eat, drink, or sleep.' Bunyan, in this description, is supposed to have taken the picture from himself. But too much may be made of this. He was thinking, perhaps, of what he might have been if God's grace had not preserved him. He himself was saved. Badman is represented as given over from the first. Anecdotes, however, are told of contemporary providential judgments upon swearers, which had much impressed Bunyan. One was of a certain Dorothy Mately, a woman whose business was to wash rubbish at the Derby lead mines. Dorothy (it was in the year when Bunyan was first imprisoned), had stolen twopence from the coat of a boy who was working near her. When the boy taxed her with having robbed him, she wished the ground might swallow her up if she had ever touched his money. Presently after, some children who were watching her, saw a movement in the bank on which she was standing. They called to her to take care, but it was too late. The bank fell in, and she was carried down along with it. A man ran to help her, but the sides of the pit were crumbling round her : a large stone fell on her head ; the rubbish followed, and she was overwhelmed. When she was dug out afterwards, the pence were found in her pocket. Bunyan was perfectly satisfied that her death was supernatural. To discover miracles is not peculiar to Catholics. They will be found wherever there is an active belief in immediate providential government.

Those more cautious in forming their conclusions will think, perhaps, that the woman was working above some shaft in the mine, that the crust had suddenly broken, and that it would equally have fallen in when gravitation required it to fall, if Dorothy Mately had been a saint. They will remember the words about the Tower of Siloam. But to return to Badman.

His father, being unable to manage so unpromising a child, bound him out as an apprentice. The master to whom he was assigned was as good a man as the father could find : upright, Godfearing, and especially considerate of his servants. He never worked them too hard. He left them time to read and pray. He admitted no light or mischievous books within his doors. He was not one of those whose religion 'hung as a cloke in his house, and was never seen on him when he went abroad.' His household was as well fed and cared for as himself, and he required nothing of others of which he did not set them an example in his own person.

This man did his best to reclaim young Badman, and was particularly kind to him. But his exertions were thrown away. The good-for-nothing youth read filthy romances on the sly. He fell asleep in church, or made eyes at the pretty girls. He made acquaintance with low companions. He became profligate, got drunk at alehouses, sold his master's property to get money, or stole it out of the cashbox. Thrice he ran away and was taken back again. The third time he was allowed to go. 'The House of Correction would have been the most fit for him, but thither his master was loath to send him, for the love he bore his father.'

He was again apprenticed ; this time to a master like himself. Being wicked he was given over to wickedness. The ways of it were not altogether pleasant. He was fed worse and he was worked harder than he had been before; when he stole, or neglected his business, he was beaten. He liked his new place, however, better than the old. 'At least, there was no godliness in the house, which he hated worst of all.'

So far, Bunyan's hero was travelling the usual road of the Idle Apprentice, and the gallows would have been the commonplace ending of it. But this would not have

answered Bunyan's purpose. He wished to represent the
good-for-nothing character, under the more instructive aspect of worldly success, which bad men may arrive at as
well as good, if they are prudent and cunning. Bunyan
gives his hero every chance. He submits him from the
first to the best influences; he creates opportunities for
repentance at every stage of a long career—opportunities
which the reprobate nature cannot profit by, yet increases
its guilt by neglecting.

Badman's term being out, his father gives him money
and sets him up as a tradesman on his own account. Mr.
Attentive considers this to have been a mistake. Mr.
Wiseman answers that even in the most desperate cases,
kindness in parents is more likely to succeed than severity,
and if it fails they will have the less to reproach themselves with. The kindness is, of course, thrown away.
Badman continues a loose blackguard, extravagant, idle
and dissolute. He comes to the edge of ruin. His situation obliges him to think; and now the interest of the
story begins. He must repair his fortune by some means
or other. The easiest way is by marriage. There was a
young orphan lady in the neighbourhood, who was well
off and her own mistress. She was a 'professor' eagerly
given to religion, and not so wise as she ought to have
been. Badman pretends to be converted. He reforms,
or seems to reform. He goes to meeting, sings hymns,
adopts the most correct form of doctrine, tells the lady
that he does not want her money, but that he wants a
companion who will go with him along the road to
Heaven. He was plausible, good-looking, and, to all
appearance, as absorbed as herself in the one thing need-
ful. The congregation warn her, but to no purpose. She

marries him, and finds what she has done too late. In her fortune he has all that he wanted. He swears at her, treats her brutally, brings prostitutes into his house, laughs at her religion, and at length orders her to give it up. When she refuses, Bunyan introduces a special feature of the times, and makes Badman threaten to turn informer, and bring her favourite minister to gaol. The informers were the natural but most accursed products of the Conventicle Acts. Popular abhorrence relieved itself by legends of the dreadful judgments which had overtaken these wretches.

In St. Neots an informer was bitten by a dog. The wound gangrened and the flesh rotted off his bones. In Bedford 'there was one W. S.' (Bunyan probably knew him too well), 'a man of very wicked life, and he, when there seemed to be countenance given to it, would needs turn informer. Well, so he did, and was as diligent in his business as most of them could be. He would watch at nights, climb trees and range the woods of days, if possible to find out the meeters, for then they were forced to meet in the fields. Yea, he would curse them bitterly, and swore most fearfully what he would do to them when he found them. Well, after he had gone on like a Bedlam in his course awhile, and had done some mischief to the people, he was stricken by the hand of God. He was taken with a faltering in his speech, a weakness in the back sinews of his neck, that ofttimes he held up his head by strength of hand. After this his speech went quite away, and he could speak no more than a swine or a bear. Like one of them he would gruntle and make an ugly noise, according as he was offended or pleased, or would have anything done. He walked about till God had made a sufficient spectacle of his judgments for his sin, and then, on a sudden, he was stricken, and died miserably.'

Badman, says Mr. Wiseman, 'had malice enough in his heart' to turn informer, but he was growing prudent and had an eye to the future.   As a tradesman he had to live by his neighbours. He knew that they would not forgive him, so 'he had that wit in his anger that he did it not.' Nothing else was neglected to make the unfortunate wife miserable.   She bore him seven children, also typical figures.   'One was a very gracious child, that loved its mother dearly.   This child Mr. Badman could not abide, and it oftenest felt the weight of its father's fingers. Three were as bad as himself.   The others that remained became a kind of mongrel professors, not so bad as their father nor so good as their mother, but betwixt them both.   They had their mother's notions and their father's actions.   Their father did not like them because they had their mother's tongue.   Their mother did not like them because they had their father's heart and life, nor were they fit company for good or bad. They were forced with Esau to join in affinity with Ishmael, to wit, to look out for a people that were hypocrites like themselves, and with them they matched and lived and died.'

Badman meanwhile, with the help of his wife's fortune, grew into an important person, and his character becomes a curious study.   'He went,' we are told, 'to school with the Devil, from his childhood to the end of his life.'   He was shrewd in matters of business, began to extend his operations, and 'drove a great trade.' He carried a double face.   He was evil with the evil.   He pretended to be good with the good.   In religion he affected to be a freethinker, careless of death and judgment, and ridiculing those who feared them 'as frighted with unseen bugbears.'

But he wore a mask when it suited him, and admired himself for the ease with which he could assume whatever aspect was convenient. 'I can be religious and irreligious,' he said; 'I can be anything or nothing. I can swear and speak against swearing. I can lie and speak against lying. I can drink, wench, be unclean, and defraud, and not be troubled for it. I can enjoy myself and am master of my own ways, not they of me. This I have attained with much study, care, and pains.' 'An Atheist Badman was, if such a thing as an Atheist could be. He was not alone in that mystery. There was abundance of men of the same mind and the same principle. He was only an arch or chief one among them.'

Mr. Badman now took to speculation, which Bunyan's knowledge of business enabled him to describe with instructive minuteness. His adventures were on a large scale, and by some mistakes and by personal extravagance he had nearly ruined himself a second time. In this condition he discovered a means, generally supposed to be a more modern invention, of 'getting money by hatfuls.'

'He gave a sudden and great rush into several men's debts to the value of four or five thousand pounds, driving at the same time a very great trade by selling many things for less than they cost him, to get him custom and blind his creditors' eyes. When he had well feathered his nest with other men's goods and money, after a little while he breaks; while he had by craft and knavery made so sure of what he had, that his creditors could not touch a penny. He sends mournful sugared letters to them, desiring them not to be severe with him, for he bore towards all men an honest mind, and would pay them as far as he was able. He talked of the greatness of the taxes, the badness of the times, his losses by bad debts, and he brought them to a

composition to take five shillings in the pound. His release was signed and sealed, and Mr. Badman could now
put his head out of doors again, and be a better man than
when he shut up shop by several thousands of pounds.'

Twice or three times he repeated the same trick with
equal success. It is likely enough that Bunyan was
drawing from life and perhaps from a member of his own
congregation ; for he says that ' he had known a professor
do it.' He detested nothing so much as sham religion
which was put on as a pretence. ' A professor,' he ex-
claims, ' and practise such villanies as these ! Such an
one is not worthy the name. Go professors, go—leave off
profession unless you will lead your lives according to
your profession. Better never profess than make profession a stalking horse to sin, deceit, the devil, and hell.'

Bankruptcy was not the only art by which Badman
piled up his fortune. The seventeenth century was not
so far behind us as we sometimes persuade ourselves.
' He dealt by deceitful weights and measures. He kept
weights to buy by and weights to sell by, measures to buy
by and measures to sell by. Those he bought by were
too big, and those he sold by were too little. If he had
to do with other men's weights and measures, he could
use a thing called sleight of hand. He had the art besides to misreckon men in their accounts, whether by
weight or measure or money ; and if a question was made
of his faithful dealing, he had his servants ready that
would vouch and swear to his look or word. He would
sell goods that cost him not the best price by far, for as
much as he sold his best of all for. He had also a trick
to mingle his commodity, that that which was bad might
go off with the least mistrust. If any of his customers
paid him money, he would call for payment a second

time, and if they could not produce good and sufficient
ground of the payment, a hundred to one but they paid it
again.'

'To buy in the cheapest market and sell in the
dearest' was Mr. Badman's common rule in business.
According to modern political economy, it is the cardinal
principle of wholesome trade. In Bunyan's opinion it
was knavery in disguise, and certain to degrade and
demoralise everyone who acted upon it. Bunyan had
evidently thought on the subject. Mr. Attentive is made
to object :—

'But you know that there is no settled price set by
God upon any commodity that is bought or sold under the
sun; but all things that we buy and sell do ebb and flow
as to price like the tide. How then shall a man of tender
conscience do, neither to wrong the seller, buyer, nor himself in the buying and selling of commodities ?'

Mr. Wiseman answers in the spirit of our old Acts of
Parliament, before political economy was invented :—

'Let a man have conscience towards God, charity to
his neighbours, and moderation in dealing. Let the
tradesman consider that there is not that in great gettings
and in abundance which the most of men do suppose; for
all that a man has over and above what serves for his present necessity and supply, serves only to feed the lusts of
the eye. Be thou confident that God's eyes are upon thy
ways; that He marks them, writes them down, and seals
them up in a bag against the time to come. Be sure that
thou rememberest that thou knowest not the day of thy
death. Thou shalt have nothing that thou mayest so
much as carry away in thy hand. Guilt shall go with
thee if thou hast gotten thy substance dishonestly, and
they to whom thou shalt leave it shall receive it to their

hurt. These things duly considered, I will shew thee how thou should'st live in the practical part of this art. Art thou to buy or sell? If thou sellest do not commend. If thou buyest do not dispraise, any otherwise but to give the thing that thou hast to do with its just value and worth. Art thou a seller and do things grow cheap? set not thy hand to help or hold them up higher. Art thou a buyer and do things grow dear? use no cunning or deceitful language to pull them down. Leave things to the Providence of God, and do thou with moderation submit to his hand. Hurt not thy neighbour by crying out Scarcity, scarcity! beyond the truth of things. Especially take heed of doing this by way of a prognostic for time to come. This wicked thing may be done by hoarding up (food) when the hunger and necessity of the poor calls for it. If things rise do thou be grieved. Be also moderate in all thy sellings, and be sure let the poor have a pennyworth, and sell thy corn to those who are in necessity; which thou wilt do when thou showest mercy to the poor in thy selling to him, and when thou undersellest the market for his sake because he is poor. This is to buy and sell with a good conscience. The buyer thou wrongest not, thy conscience thou wrongest not, thyself thou wrongest not, for God will surely recompense with thee.'

These views of Bunyan's are at issue with modern science, but his principles and ours are each adjusted to the objects of desire which good men in those days and good men in ours have respectively set before themselves. If wealth means money, as it is now assumed to do, Bunyan is wrong and modern science right. If wealth means moral welfare, then those who aim at it will do well to follow Bunyan's advice. It is to be feared that this part of his doctrine is less frequently dwelt upon by those who profess to admire and follow him, than the theory of imputed righteousness or justification by faith.

Mr. Badman by his various ingenuities became a wealthy man. His character as a tradesman could not have been a secret from his neighbours, but money and success coloured it over. The world spoke well of him. He became 'proud and haughty,' took part in public affairs, 'counted himself as wise as the wisest in the country, as good as the best, and as beautiful as he that had the most of it.' 'He took great delight in praising himself, and as much in the praises that others gave him.' 'He could not abide that any should think themselves above him, or that their wit and personage should be by others set before his.' He had an objection, nevertheless, to being called proud, and when Mr. Attentive asked why, his companion answered with a touch which reminds us of De Foe, that 'Badman *did not tell him the reason.* He supposed it to be that which was common to all vile persons. They loved their vice, but cared not to bear its name.' Badman said he was unwilling to seem singular and fantastical, and in this way he justified his expensive and luxurious way of living. Singularity of all kinds he affected to dislike, and for that reason his special pleasure was to note the faults of professors. 'If he could get anything by the end that had scandal in it, if it did but touch professors, however falsely reported, oh, then he would glory, laugh and be glad, and lay it upon the whole party. Hang these rogues, he would say, there is not a barrel better herring in all the holy brotherhood of them. Like to like, quoth the Devil to the collier. This is your precise crew, and then he would send them all home with a curse.'

Thus Bunyan developed his specimen scoundrel, till he brought him to the high altitudes of worldly prosperity; skilful in every villanous art, skilful equally in keeping out of the law's hands, and feared, admired and respected by all his neighbours.   The reader who desires to see Providence vindicated would now expect to find him detected in some crimes by which justice could lay hold, and poetical retribution fall upon him in the midst of his triumph.   An inferior artist would certainly have allowed his story to end in this way.   But Bunyan, satisfied though he was that dramatic judgments did overtake offenders in this world with direct and startling appropriateness, was yet aware that it was often otherwise, and that the worst fate which could be inflicted on a completely worthless person was to allow him to work out his career unvisited by any penalties which might have disturbed his conscience and occasioned his amendment. He chose to make his story natural, and to confine himself to natural machinery.   The judgment to come Mr. Badman laughed at ' as old woman's fable,' but his courage lasted only as long as he was well and strong.   One night as he was riding home drunk, his horse fell and he broke his leg.   ' You would not think,' says Mr. Wiseman, ' how he swore at first.   Then coming to himself, and finding he was badly hurt, he cried out, after the manner of such, Lord help me ; Lord have mercy on me ; good God deliver me, and the like.   He was picked up and taken home, where he lay some time.   In his pain he called on God, but whether it was that his sin might be pardoned and his soul saved, or whether to be rid of his pain,' Mr. Wiseman ' could not determine.'   This leads to several stories of drunkards which Bunyan clearly believed to be literally true.   Such facts or legends were the

food on which his mind had been nourished. They were
in the air which contemporary England breathed.

'I have read in Mr. Clarke's Looking-glass for Sinners,' Mr. Wiseman said, 'that upon a time a certain
drunken fellow boasted in his cups that there was neither
heaven nor hell. Also he said he believed that man had
no soul, and that for his own part he would sell his soul
to any that would buy it. Then did one of his companions buy it of him for a cup of wine, and presently
the devil, in man's shape, bought it of that man again at
the same price; and so in the presence of them all laid
hold of the soul-seller, and carried him away through the
air so that he was no more heard of.'

Again:

'There was one at Salisbury drinking and carousing
at a tavern, and he drank a health to the devil, saying
that if the devil would not come and pledge him, he could
not believe that there was either God or devil. Where-
upon his companions, stricken with fear, hastened out of
the room, and presently after, hearing a hideous noise
and smelling a stinking savour, the vintner ran into the
chamber, and coming in he missed his guest, and found
the window broken, the iron bars in it bowed and all
bloody, but the man was never heard of afterwards.'

These visitations were answers to a direct challenge of
the evil spirit's existence, and were thus easy to be ac-
counted for. But no devil came for Mr. Badman. He
clung to his unfortunate neglected wife. 'She became
his dear wife, his godly wife, his honest wife, his duck,
his dear and all.' He thought he was dying, and hell
and all its horrors rose up before him. 'Fear was in his
face, and in his tossings to and fro he would often say
I am undone, I am undone, my vile life hath undone me.'

Atheism did not help him. It never helped anyone in such extremities Mr. Wiseman said ; as he had known in another instance :—

' There was a man dwelt about twelve miles off from us,' he said, ' that had so trained up himself in his Atheistical notions, that at last he attempted to write a book against Jesus Christ and the Divine authority of the Scriptures. I think it was not printed. Well, after many days God struck him with sickness whereof he died. So being sick, and musing of his former doings, the book that he had written tore his conscience as a lion would tear a kid. Some of my friends went to see him, and as they were in his chamber one day he hastily called for pen and ink and paper, which, when it was given to him, he took it and writ to this purpose. " I such an one in such a town must go to hell fire for writing a book against Jesus Christ." He would have leaped out of the window to have killed himself, but was by them prevented of that, so he died in his bed by such a death as it was.'

Badman seemed equally miserable. But death-bed repentances, as Bunyan sensibly said, were seldom of more value than ' the howling of a dog.' The broken leg was set again. The pain of body went, and with it the pain of mind. He was assisted out of his uneasiness, says Bunyan, with a characteristic hit at the scientific views then coming into fashion, ' by his doctor,' who told him that his alarms had come ' from an affection of the brain, caused by want of sleep ; ' ' they were nothing but vapours and the effects of his distemper.' He gathered his spirits together, and became the old man once more. , His poor wife, who had believed him penitent, broke her heart, and died of the disappointment. The husband gave himself up to loose connections with abandoned women, one of whom persuaded him one day, when he was drunk, to make her a promise of marriage, and she held him to his word. Then retribution came upon him, with the coarse, commonplace, yet rigid justice which fact really deals out. The second bad wife avenged the wrongs of the first innocent wife. He was mated with a companion 'who could fit him with cursing and swearing, give him oath for oath, and curse for curse. They would fight and fly at each other like cat and dog.' In this condition—for Bunyan, before sending his hero to his account, gave him a protracted spell of earthly discomforts—they lived sixteen years together. Fortune, who had so long favoured his speculations, turned her back upon him. Between them they 'sinned all his wealth away,' and at last parted 'as poor as howlets.'

Then came the end. Badman was still in middle life, and had naturally a powerful constitution; but his 'cups and his queans' had undermined his strength. Dropsy came, and gout, with worse in his bowels, and 'on the top of them all, as the captain of the men of death that came to take him away,' consumption. Bunyan was a true artist, though he knew nothing of the rules, and was not aware that he was an artist at all. He was not to be tempted into spoiling a natural story with the melodramatic horrors of a sinner's deathbed. He had let his victim 'howl' in the usual way, when he meant him to recover. He had now simply to conduct him to the gate of the place where he was to receive the reward of his iniquities. It was enough to bring him thither still impenitent, with the grave solemnity with which a felon is taken to execution.

'As his life was full of sin,' says Mr. Wiseman, 'so his death was without repentance. He had not, in all

the time of his sickness, a sight and a sense of his sins;
but was as much at quiet as if he had never sinned in his
life: he was as secure as if he had been sinless as an
angel. When he drew near his end, there was no more
alteration in him than what was made by his disease
upon his body. He was the selfsame Mr. Badman still,
not only in name, but in condition, and that to the very
day of his death and the moment in which he died.
There seemed not to be in it to the standers by so much
as a strong struggle of nature. He died like a lamb, or,
as men call it, like a chrisom child, quietly and without
fear.'

To which end of Mr. Badman Bunyan attaches the
following remarks : ' If a wicked man, if a man who has
lived all his days in notorious sin, dies quietly, his quiet
dying is so far from being a sign of his being saved that
it is an incontestable proof of his damnation. No man
can be saved except he repents; nor can he repent that
knows not that he is a sinner : and he that knows himself to be a sinner will, I warrant him, be molested for
his knowledge before he can die quietly. I am no ad-
mirer of sick-bed repentance; for I think verily it is
seldom good for anything. But I see that he that hath
lived in sin and profaneness all his days, as Badman did,
and yet shall die quietly, that is, without repentance steps
in between his life and his death, is assuredly gone to
hell. When God would show the greatness of his anger
against sin and sinners in one word, He saith, Let them
alone ! Let them alone—that is, disturb them not.
Let them go on without control. Let the devil enjoy
them peaceably. Let him carry them out of the world
unconverted quietly. This is the sorest of judgments. I
do not say that all wicked men that are molested at their

death with a sense of sin and fear of hell do therefore go
to heaven ; for some are made to see and are left to despair.
But I say there is no surer sign of a man's damnation
than to die quietly after a sinful life, than to sin and die
with a heart that cannot repent. The opinion, therefore,
of the common people of this kind of death is frivolous
and vain.'

So ends this very remarkable story. It is extremely
interesting, merely as a picture of vulgar English life in
a provincial town such as Bedford was when Bunyan
lived there. The drawing is so good, the details so
minute, the conception so unexaggerated, that we are
disposed to believe that we must have a real history
before us. But such a supposition is only a compliment to
the skill of the composer. Bunyan's inventive faculty
was a spring that never ran dry. He had a manner, as
I said, like De Foe's, of creating the illusion that we are
reading realities, by little touches such as ' I do not
know,' ' He did not tell me this,' or the needless introduction of particulars irrelevant to the general plot such
as we always stumble on in life, and writers of fiction
usually omit. Bunyan was never prosecuted for libel by
' Badman's' relations, and the character is the correspond-
ing contrast to Christian in the ' Pilgrim's Progress,' the
pilgrim's journey being in the opposite direction to the
other place. Throughout we are on the solid earth,
amidst real experiences. No demand is made on our
credulity by Providential interpositions, except in the in-
tercalated anecdotes which do not touch the story itself.
The wicked man's career is not brought to the abrupt
or sensational issues so much in favour with ordinary didactic tale-writers. Such issues are the exception, not
the rule, and the edifying story loses its effect when the

reader turns from it to actual life, and perceives that the
majority are not punished in any such way. Bunyan con-
ceals nothing, assumes nothing, and exaggerates nothing.
He makes his bad man sharp and shrewd. He allows
sharpness and shrewdness to bring him the rewards which
such qualities in fact command. Badman is successful,
he is powerful; he enjoys all the pleasures which money
can buy; his bad wife helps him to ruin, but otherwise
he is not unhappy, and he dies in peace. Bunyan has
made him a brute, because such men do become brutes.
It is the real punishment of brutal and selfish habits.
There the figure stands; a picture of a man in the rank
of English life with which Bunyan was most familiar,
travelling along the primrose path to the everlasting
bonfire, as the way to Emmanuel's Land was through
the Slough of Despond and the Valley of the Shadow of
Death. Pleasures are to be found among the primroses,
such pleasures as a brute can be gratified by. Yet the
reader feels that even if there was no bonfire, he would
still prefer to be with Christian.

CHAPTER VIII.

THE HOLY WAR.

THE supernatural has been successfully represented in poetry, painting, or sculpture, only at particular periods of human history, and under peculiar mental conditions. The artist must himself believe in the supernatural, or his description of it will be a sham, without dignity and without credibility. He must feel himself able at the same time to treat the subject which he selects with freedom, throwing his own mind boldly into it, or he will produce, at best, the hard and stiff forms of literal tradition. When Benvenuto Cellini was preparing to make an image of the Virgin, he declares gravely that Our Lady appeared to him that he might know what she was like; and so real was the apparition that for many months after, he says that his friends when the room was dark could see a faint aureole about his head. Yet Benvenuto worked as if his own brain was partly the author of what he produced, and, like other contemporary artists, used his mistresses for his models, and was no servile copyist of phantoms seen in visions. There is a truth of the imagination, and there is a truth of fact, religion hovering between them, translating one into the other, turning natural phenomena into the activity of personal beings; or giving earthly names and habitations to mere

creatures of fancy. Imagination creates a mythology.
The priest takes it and fashions out of it a theology, a
ritual, or a sacred history. So long as the priest can
convince the world that he is dealing with literal facts,
he holds reason prisoner, and imagination is his servant.
In the twilight when dawn is coming near but has not
yet come; when the uncertain nature of the legend is
felt, though not intelligently discerned; imagination is
the first to resume its liberty; it takes possession of
its own inheritance, it dreams of its gods and demi-gods,
as Benvenuto dreamt of the Virgin, and it re-shapes
the priest's traditions in noble and beautiful forms.
Homer and the Greek dramatists would not have dared
to bring the gods upon the stage so freely, had they believed Zeus and Apollo were living persons, like the man
in the next street, who might call the poet to account for
what they were made to do and say; but neither, on the
other hand, could they have been actively conscious that
Zeus and Apollo were apparitions, which had no existence, except in their own brains.

The condition is extremely peculiar. It can exist only
in certain epochs, and in its nature is necessarily transi-
tory. Where belief is consciously gone the artist has no
reverence for his work, and therefore can inspire none. The
greatest genius in the world could not reproduce another
Athene like that of Phidias. But neither must the belief
be too complete. The poet's tongue stammers when he
would bring beings before us who, though invisible, are
awful personal existences, in whose stupendous presence
we one day expect to stand. As long as the conviction
survives that he is dealing with literal truths, he is safe
only while he follows with shoeless feet the letter of the
tradition. He dares not step beyond, lest he degrade the

Infinite to the human level, and if he is wise he prefers
to content himself with humbler subjects. A Christian
artist can represent Jesus Christ as a man because He was
a man, and because the details of the Gospel history leave
room for the imagination to work. To represent Christ
as the Eternal Son in heaven, to bring before us the
Persons of the Trinity consulting, planning, and reasoning,
to take us into their everlasting Council Chamber, as
Homer takes us into Olympus, will be possible only when
Christianity ceases to be regarded as a history of true facts.
Till then it is a trespass beyond the permitted limits,
and revolts us by the inadequacy of the result. Either
the artist fails altogether by attempting the impossible,
or those whom he addresses are themselves intellectually
injured by an unreal treatment of truths hitherto sacred.
They confound the representation with its object, and
regard the whole of it as unreal together.

These observations apply most immediately to Milton's
'Paradise Lost,' and are meant to explain the unsatisfac-
toriness of it. Milton himself was only partially eman-
cipated from the bondage of the letter; half in earth,
half 'pawing to get free' like his own lion. The war
in heaven, the fall of the rebel angels, the horrid splen-
dours of Pandemonium seem legitimate subjects for Christian poetry. They stand for something which we regard
as real, yet we are not bound to any actual opinions about
them. Satan has no claim on reverential abstinence;
and Paradise and the Fall of Man are perhaps sufficiently mythic to permit poets to take certain liberties
with them. But even so far Milton has not entirely
succeeded. His wars of the angels are shadowy. They
have no substance like the battles of Greeks and Tro-
jans, or Centaurs and Lapithæ; and Satan could not be

made interesting without touches of a nobler nature, that is, without ceasing to be the Satan of the Christian religion. But this is not his worst. When we are carried up into heaven and hear the persons of the Trinity conversing on the mischiefs which have crept into the universe, and planning remedies and schemes of salvation like Puritan divines, we turn away incredulous and resentful. Theologians may form such theories for themselves, if not wisely, yet without offence. They may study the world in which they are placed, with the light which can be thrown upon it by the book which they call the Word of God. They may form their conclusions, invent their schemes of doctrine, and commend to their flocks the interpretation of the mystery at which they have arrived. The cycles and epicycles of the Ptolemaic astronomers were imperfect hypotheses, but they were stages on which the mind could rest for a more complete examination of the celestial phenomena. But the poet does not offer us phrases and formulas; he presents to us personalities living and active, influenced by emotions and reasoning from premises; and when the unlimited and incomprehensible Being whose attributes are infinite, of whom from the inadequacy of our ideas we can only speak in negatives, is brought on the stage to talk like an ordinary man, we feel that Milton has mistaken the necessary limits of his art.

When Faust claims affinity with the Erdgeist, the spirit tells him to seek affinities with beings which he can comprehend. The commandment which forbade the representation of God in a bodily form, forbids the poet equally to make God describe his feelings and his purposes. Where the poet would create a character he must himself comprehend it first to its inmost fibre. He can-

not comprehend his own Creator. Admire as we may
'Paradise Lost;' try as we may to admire 'Paradise
Regained;' acknowledge as we must the splendour of the
imagery and the stately march of the verse; there comes
upon us irresistibly a sense of the unfitness of the subject for Milton's treatment of it. If the story which he
tells us is true, it is too momentous to be played with in
poetry. We prefer to hear it in plain prose, with a
minimum of ornament and the utmost possible precision
of statement. Milton himself had not arrived at thinking
it to be a legend, a picture like a Greek Mythology.
His poem falls between two modes of treatment and two
conceptions of truth; we wonder, we recite, we applaud,
but something comes in between our minds and a full
enjoyment, and it will not satisfy us better as time
goes on.

The same objection applies to 'The Holy War' of Bunyan. It is as I said, a people's version of the same series
of subjects—the creation of man, the fall of man, his
redemption, his ingratitude, his lapse, and again his
restoration. The chief figures are the same, the action
is the same, though more varied and complicated, and
the general effect is unsatisfactory from the same cause.
Prose is less ambitious than poetry. There is an absence
of attempts at grand effects. There is no effort after
sublimity, and there is consequently a lighter sense of
incongruity in the failure to reach it. On the other hand,
there is the greater fulness of detail so characteristic of
Bunyan's manner; and fulness of detail on a theme so far
beyond our understanding is as dangerous as vague gran-
diloquence. In 'The Pilgrim's Progress' we are among
genuine human beings. The reader knows the road
too well which Christian follows. He has struggled with

him in the Slough of Despond. He has shuddered with
him in the Valley of the Shadow of Death. He has
groaned with him in the dungeons of Doubting Castle.
He has encountered on his journey the same fellow-
travellers. Who does not know Mr. Pliable, Mr. Obstinate, Mr. Facing-both-ways, Mr. Feeble Mind, and all
the rest? They are representative realities, flesh of our
flesh and bone of our bone. 'If we prick them they
bleed, if we tickle them they laugh,' or they make us laugh.
'They are warmed and cooled by the same winter and
summer' as we are. The human actors in 'The Holy
War' are parts of men—special virtues, special vices:
allegories in fact as well as in name, which all Bunyan's
genius can only occasionally substantiate into persons.
The plot of 'The Pilgrim's Progress' is simple. 'The Holy
War' is prolonged through endless vicissitudes, with a
doubtful issue after all, and the incomprehensibility of
the Being who allows Satan to defy him so long and so
successfully is unpleasantly and harshly brought home to
us. True it is so in life. Evil remains after all that has
been done for us. But life is confessedly a mystery. 'The
Holy War' professes to interpret the mystery, and only
restates the problem in a more elaborate form. Man
Friday on reading it would have asked even more em-
phatically, 'Why God not kill the Devil?' and Robinson
Crusoe would have found no assistance in answering him.
For these reasons, I cannot agree with Macaulay in
thinking that if there had been no 'Pilgrim's Progress,'
'The Holy War' would have been the first of religious
allegories. We may admire the workmanship, but the
same undefined sense of unreality which pursues us
through Milton's epic would have interfered equally with
the acceptance of this. The question to us is if the facts

are true. If true they require no allegories to touch
either our hearts or our intellects.

'The Holy War' would have entitled Bunyan to a
place among the masters of English literature. It would
never have made his name a household word in every
English-speaking family on the globe.

The story which I shall try to tell in an abridged
form is introduced by a short prefatory poem. Works
of fancy, Bunyan tells us, are of many sorts, according
to the author's humour. For himself he says to his
reader :

> I have something else to do
> Than write vain stories thus to trouble you.
> What here I say some men do know too well ;
> They can with tears and joy the story tell.
> The town of Mansoul is well known to many,
> Nor are her troubles doubted of by any
> That are acquainted with those histories
> That Mansoul and her wars anatomize.
>
> Then lend thine ears to what I do relate
> Touching the town of Mansoul and her state,
> How she was lost, took captive, made a slave,
> And how against him set that should her save,
> Yea, how by hostile ways she did oppose
> Her Lord and with his enemy did close,
> For they are true ; he that will them deny
> Must needs the best of records vilify.
>
> For my part, I myself was in the town
> Both when 'twas set up and when pulling down.
> I saw Diabolus in his possession,
> And Mansoul also under his oppression :
> Yea I was there when she him owned for Lord,
> And to him did submit with one accord.
>
> When Mansoul trampled upon things divine,
> And wallowed in filth as doth a swine,

When she betook herself unto his arms,
Fought her Emmanuel, despised his charms;
Then was I there and did rejoice to see
Diabolus and Mansoul so agree.

Let no man count me then a fable maker,
Nor make my name or credit a partaker
Of their derision.   What is here in view
Of mine own knowledge I dare say is true.

At setting out we are introduced into the famous con-
tinent of ‘ Universe,’ a large and spacious country lying
between the two poles—‘ the people of it not all of one
complexion nor yet of one language, mode or way of
religion ; but differing as much as the planets themselves, some right, some wrong, even as it may happen to
be.’

In this country of ‘ Universe’ was a fair and delicate
town and corporation called ‘ Mansoul,’ a town for its
building so curious, for its situation so commodious, for
its privileges so advantageous, that with reference to its
original (state) there was not its equal under heaven.
The first founder was Shaddai, who built it for his own
delight.   In the midst of the town was a famous and
stately palace which Shaddai intended for himself.[1]   He
had no intention of allowing strangers to intrude there.
And the peculiarity of the place was that the walls of
Mansoul [2] could never be broken down or hurt unless
the townsmen consented.   Mansoul had five gates which
in like manner could only be forced if those within
allowed it.   These gates were Eargate, Eyegate, Mouthgate, Nosegate, and Feelgate.   Thus provided, Mansoul

---

[1] Bunyan says in a marginal note, that by this palace he
means the heart.

[2] The body.

was at first all that its founder could desire. It had the most excellent laws in the world. There was not a rogue or a rascal inside its whole precincts. The inhabitants were all true men.

Now there was a certain giant named Diabolus—king of the blacks or negroes, as Bunyan noticeably calls them—the negroes standing for sinners or fallen angels. Diabolus had once been a servant of Shaddai, one of the chief in his territories. Pride and ambition had led him to aspire to the crown which was settled on Shaddai's Son. He had formed a conspiracy and planned a revolution. Shaddai and his Son, 'being all eye,' easily detected the plot. Diabolus and his crew were bound in chains, banished, and thrown into a pit, there to 'abide for ever.' This was their sentence; but out of the pit, in spite of it, they in some way contrived to escape. They ranged about full of malice against Shaddai, and looking for means to injure him. They came at last on Mansoul. They determined to take it, and called a council to consider how it could best be done. Diabolus was aware of the condition that no one could enter without the inhabitants' consent. Alecto, Apollyon, Beelzebub, Lucifer (Pagan and Christian demons intermixed indifferently) gave their several opinions. Diabolus at length at Lucifer's suggestion decided to assume the shape of one of the creatures over which Mansoul had dominion; and he selected as the fittest that of a snake, which at that time was in great favour with the people as both harmless and wise.

The population of Mansoul were simple, innocent folks who believed everything that was said to them. Force, however, might be necessary as well as cunning, and the Tisiphone, a fury of the Lakes, was required to assist.

The attempt was to be made at Eargate. A certain
Captain Resistance was in charge of this gate, whom
Diabolus feared more than any one in the place. Tisiphone
was to shoot him.

The plans being all laid, Diabolus in his snake's dress
approached the wall, accompanied by one 'Ill Pause,' a
famous orator, the Fury following behind. He asked
for a parley with the heads of the town. Captain
Resistance, two of the great nobles, Lord 'Innocent,' and
Lord 'Will be Will,' with Mr. Conscience, the Recorder,
and Lord Understanding, the Lord Mayor, came to the
gate to see what he wanted. Lord 'Will be Will' plays
a prominent part in the drama both for good and evil.
He is neither Free Will, nor Wilfulness, nor Inclination,
but the quality which metaphysicians and theologians
agree in describing as 'the Will.' 'The Will' simply—a
subtle something of great importance ; but what it is
they have never been able to explain.

Lord Will be Will inquired Diabolus's business. Diabolus, 'meek as a lamb,' said he was a neighbour of theirs.
He had observed with distress that they were living in a
state of slavery, and he wished to help them to be free.
Shaddai was no doubt a great prince, but he was an
arbitrary despot. There was no liberty where the laws
were unreasonable, and Shaddai's laws were the reverse
of reasonable. They had a fruit growing among them,
in Mansoul, which they had but to eat to become wise.
Knowledge was well known to be the best of possessions.
Knowledge was freedom ; ignorance was bondage ; and
yet Shaddai had forbidden them to touch this precious
fruit.

At that moment Captain Resistance fell dead, pierced
by an arrow from Tisiphone. Ill Pause made a flowing

speech, in the midst of which Lord Innocent fell also,
either through a blow from Diabolus, or 'overpowered by
the stinking breath of the old villain Ill Pause.' The
people flew upon the apple tree; Eargate and Eyegate were
thrown open, and Diabolus was invited to come in; when
at once he became King of Mansoul and established himself in the castle.[1]

The magistrates were immediately changed. Lord
Understanding ceased to be Lord Mayor. Mr. Conscience
was no longer left as Recorder. Diabolus built up a wall
in front of Lord Understanding's palace, and shut off the
light, 'so that till Mansoul was delivered the old Lord
Mayor was rather an impediment than an advantage to that
famous town.' Diabolus tried long to bring 'Conscience'
over to his side, but never quite succeeded. The Recorder
became greatly corrupted, but he could not be prevented
from now and then remembering Shaddai; and when the
fit was on him he would shake the town with his ex-
clamations. Diabolus therefore had to try other methods
with him. 'He had a way to make the old gentleman
when he was merry unsay and deny what in his fits he
had affirmed, and this was the next way to make him
ridiculous and to cause that no man should regard him.'
To make all secure Diabolus often said, 'Oh, Mansoul,
consider that, notwithstanding the old gentleman's rage
and the rattle of his high thundering words, you hear
nothing of Shaddai himself.' The Recorder had pretended
that the voice of the Lord was speaking in him. Had
this been so, Diabolus argued that the Lord would have
done more than speak. 'Shaddai,' he said, 'valued not
the loss nor the rebellion of Mansoul, nor would he
trouble himself with calling his town to a reckoning.'

[1] The heart.

In this way the Recorder came to be generally hated, and more than once the people would have destroyed him. Happily his house was a castle near the waterworks. When the rabble pursued him, he would pull up the sluices,[1] let in the flood, and drown all about him.

Lord Will be Will, on the other hand, 'as high born as any in Mansoul,' became Diabolus's principal minister. He had been the first to propose admitting Diabolus, and he was made Captain of the Castle, Governor of the Wall, and Keeper of the Gates. Will be Will had a clerk named Mr. Mind, a man every way like his master, and Mansoul was thus brought 'under the lusts' of Will and Intellect. Mr. Mind had in his house some old rent and torn parchments of the law of Shaddai. The Recorder had some more in his study; but to these Will be Will paid no attention, and surrounded himself with officials who were all in Diabolus's interest. He had as deputy one Mr. Affection, 'much debauched in his principles, so that he was called Vile Affection.' Vile Affection married Mr. Mind's daughter, Carnal Lust, by whom he had three sons—Impudent, Black Mouth, and Hate Reproof; and three daughters—Scorn Truth, Slight Good, and Revenge. All traces of Shaddai were now swept away. His image, which had stood in the market-place, was taken down, and an artist called Mr. No Truth was employed to set up the image of Diabolus in place of it. Lord Lustings—'who never savoured good, but evil'—was chosen for the new Lord Mayor. Mr. Forget Good was appointed Recorder. There were new burgesses and aldermen, all with appropriate names, for which Bunyan was never at a loss— Mr. Incredulity, Mr. Haughty, Mr. Swearing, Mr. Hardheart, Mr. Pitiless, Mr. Fury, Mr. No Truth, Mr. Stand

---

[1] Fears.

to Lies, Mr. Falsepeace, Mr. Drunkenness, Mr. Cheating,
Mr. Atheism, and another; thirteen of them in all. Mr.
Incredulity was the eldest, Mr. Atheism the youngest in
the company—a shrewd and correct arrangement. Diabolus, on his part, set to work to fortify Mansoul. He
built three fortresses—'The Hold of Defiance' at Eyegate,
that the light might be darkened there;' 'Midnight
Hold' near the old Castle, to keep Mansoul from knowledge of itself; and 'Sweet Sin Hold' in the market-
place, that there might be no desire of good there. These
strongholds being established and garrisoned, Diabolus
thought that he had made his conquest secure.

So far the story runs on firmly and clearly. It is
vivid, consistent in itself, and held well within the limits
of human nature and experience. But, like Milton, Bunyan
is now, by the exigencies of the situation, forced upon more
perilous ground. He carries us into the presence of
Shaddai himself, at the time when the loss of Mansoul was
reported in heaven.

The king, his son, his high lords, his chief captains and
nobles were all assembled to hear. There was universal
grief, in which the king and his son shared or rather seemed
to share—for at once the drama of the Fall of mankind becomes no better than a Mystery Play. 'Shaddai and his
son had foreseen it all long before, and had provided for
the relief of Mansoul, though they told not everybody
thereof—but because they would have a share in condoling
of the misery of Mansoul they did, and that at the rate
of the highest degree, bewail the losing of Mansoul'—
'thus to show their love and compassion.'

'Paradise Lost' was published at the time that Bunyan
wrote this passage. If he had not seen it, the coincidences
of treatment are singularly curious. It is equally singular,

if he had seen it, that Milton should not here at least have
taught him to avoid making the Almighty into a stage
actor.   The Father and Son consult how ' to do what they
had designed before.'   They decide that at a certain time,
which they preordain, the Son, ' a sweet and comely person,'
shall make a journey into the Universe and lay a foundation there for Mansoul's deliverance.   Milton offends in
the scene less than Bunyan ; but Milton cannot persuade
us that it is one which should have been represented by
either of them.   They should have left ' plans of salvation ' to eloquent orators in the pulpit.

Though the day of deliverance by the method proposed
was as yet far off, the war against Diabolus was to be
commenced immediately.   The Lord Chief Secretary was
ordered to put in writing Shaddai's intentions, and cause
them to be published.[1]   Mansoul, it was announced, was
to be put into a better condition than it was in before
Diabolus took it.

The report of the Council in Heaven was brought to
Diabolus, who took his measures accordingly, Lord Will he
Will standing by him and executing all his directions
Mansoul was forbidden to read Shaddai's proclamation.
Diabolus imposed a great oath on the townspeople never to
desert him ; he believed that if they entered into a covenant
of this kind Shaddai could not absolve them from it.
They ' swallowed the engagement as if it had been a sprat
in the mouth of a whale.'   Being now Diabolus's trusty
children, he gave them leave ' to do whatever their appetites prompted to do.'   They would thus involve themselves in all kinds of wickedness, and Shaddai's son ' being
Holy ' would be less likely to interest himself for them.
When they had in this way put themselves, as Diabolus

----

[1] The Scriptures.

hoped, beyond reach of mercy, he informed them that Shaddai was raising an army to destroy the town. No quarter would be given, and unless they defended themselves like men they would all be made slaves. Their spirit being roused, he armed them with the shield of unbelief, ' calling into question the truth of the Word.' He gave them a helmet of hope—' hope of doing well at last, whatever lives they might lead '; for a breastplate a heart as hard as iron, ' most necessary for all that hated Shaddai ;' and another piece of most excellent armour, ' a drunken and prayerless spirit that scorned to cry for mercy.' Shaddai on his side had also prepared his forces. He will not as yet send his son. The first expedition was to fail and was meant to fail. The object was to try whether Mansoul would return to obedience. And yet Shaddai knew that it would not return to obedience. Bunyan was too ambitious to explain the inexplicable. Fifty thousand warriors were collected, all chosen by Shaddai himself. There were four leaders—Captain Boanerges, Captain Conviction, Captain Judgment, and Captain Execution— the martial saints, with whom Macaulay thinks Bunyan made acquaintance when he served, if serve he did, with Fairfax. The bearings on their banners were three black thunderbolts—the Book of the Law, wide open, with a flame of fire bursting from it; a burning, fiery furnace; and a fruitless tree with an axe at its root. These emblems represent the terrors of Mount Sinai, the covenant of works which was not to prevail.

The captains come to the walls of Mansoul, and summon the town to surrender. Their words ' beat against Eargate, but without force to break it open.' The new officials answer the challenge with defiance. Lord Incredulity knows not by what right Shaddai invades their country.   Lord Will be Will and Mr. Forget Good warn them to be off before they rouse Diabolus.   The townspeople ring the bells and dance on the walls. Will be Will double-bars the gates.   Bunyan's genius is at its best in scenes of this kind.   'Old Mr. Prejudice, with sixty deaf men,' is appointed to take charge of Eargate.   At Eargate, too, are planted two guns, called Highmind, and Heady, 'cast in the earth by Diabolus's head founder, whose name was Mr. Puffup.'

The fighting begins, but the covenant of works makes little progress.   Shaddai's captains, when advancing on Mansoul, had fallen in with 'three young fellows of pro-mising appearance' who volunteered to go with them— Mr. Tradition, Mr. Human Wisdom, and Mr. Man's Invention.'   They were allowed to join, and were placed in positions of trust, the captains of the covenant being apparently wanting in discernment.   They were taken prisoners in the first skirmish, and immediately changed sides and went over to Diabolus.   More battles follow. The roof of the Lord Mayor's house is beaten in.   The law is not wholly ineffectual.   Six of the Aldermen, the grosser moral sins—Swearing, Stand to Lies, Drunken-ness, Cheating, and others—are overcome and killed. Diabolus grows uneasy and loses his sleep.   Old Conscience begins to talk again.   A party forms in the town in favour of surrender, and Mr. Parley is sent to Eargate to treat for terms.   The spiritual sins—False Peace, Un-belief, Haughtiness, Atheism—are still unsubdued and vigorous.   The conditions offered are that Incredulity, Forget Good, and Will be Will shall retain their offices; Mansoul shall be continued in all the liberties which it en-joys under Diabolus; and a further touch is added which shows how little Bunyan sympathised with modern notions of the beauty of self-government.   No new law or officer shall have any power in Mansoul without the people's consent.

Boanerges will agree to no conditions with rebels. Incredulity and Will be Will advise the people to stand by their rights, and refuse to submit to 'unlimited' power.   The war goes on, and Incredulity is made Diabolus's universal deputy.   Conscience and Understanding, the old Recorder and Mayor, raise a mutiny, and there is a fight in the streets.   Conscience is knocked down by a Diabolonian called 'Mr. Benumming.' Understanding had a narrow escape from being shot. On the other hand Mr. Mind, who had come over to the Conservative side, laid about bravely, tumbled old Mr. Prejudice into the dirt, and kicked him where he lay.   Even Will be Will seemed to be wavering in his allegiance to Diabolus.   'He smiled and did not seem to take one side more than another.'   The rising, however, is put down —Understanding and Conscience are imprisoned, and Mansoul hardens its heart, chiefly 'being in dread of slavery,' and thinking liberty too fine a thing to be surrendered.

Shaddai's four captains find that they can do no more. The covenant of works will not answer.   They send home a petition, 'by the hand of that good man Mr. Love to Mansoul,' to beg that some new general may come to lead them.   The preordained time has now arrived, and Emmanuel himself is to take the command.   He, too, selects his captains—Credence and Good Hope, Charity, and Innocence, and Patience; and the captains have their squires, the counterparts of themselves—Promise and Expectation, Pitiful, Harmless, and Suffer Long. Emmanuel's armour shines like the sun.   He has forty-

four battering rams and twenty-two slings—the sixty-
six books of the Bible—each made of pure gold.　He
throws up mounds and trenches, and arms them with his
rams, five of the largest being planted on Mount
Hearken, over against Eargate.　Bunyan was too reverent
to imitate the Mystery Plays, and introduce a Mount
Calvary with the central sacrifice upon it.　The sacrifice
is supposed to have been already offered elsewhere.
Emmanuel offers mercy to Mansoul, and when it is rejected he threatens judgment and terror.　Diabolus,
being wiser than man, is made to know that his hour is
approaching.　He goes in person to Mouthgate to protest
and remonstrate.　He asks why Emmanuel is come to
torment him.　Mansoul has disowned Shaddai and sworn
allegiance to himself.　He begs Emmanuel to leave him to
rule his own subjects in peace.

Emmanuel tells him 'he is a thief and a liar.'
'When,' Emmanuel is made to say, 'Mansoul sinned by
hearkening to thy lie, I put in and became a surety to my
Father, body for body, soul for soul, that I would make
amends for Mansoul's transgressions, and my Father did
accept thereof.　So when the time appointed was come, I
gave body for body, soul for soul, life for life, blood for
blood, and so redeemed my beloved Mansoul.　My
Father's law and justice, that were both concerned in the
threatening upon transgression, are both now satisfied,
and very well content that Mansoul should be delivered.'

Even against its deliverers, Mansoul was defended by
the original condition of its constitution.　There was no
way into it but through the gates.　Diabolus, feeling that
Emmanuel still had difficulties before him, withdrew from
the wall, and sent a messenger, Mr. Loth to Stoop, to offer
alternative terms, to one or other of which he thought

Emmanuel might consent.   Emmanuel might be titular
sovereign of all Mansoul, if Diabolus might keep the
administration of part of it.   If this could not be,
Diabolus requested to be allowed to reside in Mansoul as a
private person.   If Emmanuel insisted on his own personal
exclusion, at least he expected that his friends and kindred
might continue to live there, and that he himself might
now and then write them letters, and send them presents
and messages, ' in remembrance of the merry times they
had enjoyed together.'   Finally, he would like to be consulted occasionally when any difficulties arose in Mansoul.

It will be seen that in the end Mansoul was, in
fact, left liable to communications from Diabolus very
much of this kind.   Emmanuel's answer, however, is a
peremptory No.   Diabolus must take himself away, and
no more must be heard of him.   Seeing that there was no
other resource, Diabolus resolves to fight it out.   There is
a great battle under the walls, with some losses on Emmanuel's side, even Captain Conviction receiving three
wounds in the mouth.   The shots from the gold slings
mow down whole ranks of Diabolonians.   Mr. Love
no Good and Mr. Ill Pause are wounded.   Old
Prejudice and Mr. Anything run away.   Lord Will be
Will, who still fought for Diabolus, was never so daunted
in his life : ' he was hurt in the leg, and limped.'

Diabolus, when the fight was over, came again to the
gate with fresh proposals to Emmanuel.   ' I,' he said, ' will
persuade Mansoul to receive thee for their Lord, and I
know that they will do it the sooner when they understand that I am thy deputy.   I will show them wherein
they have erred, and that transgression stands in the way
to life.   I will show them the Holy law to which they

must conform, even that which they have broken. I will
press upon them the necessity of a reformation according
to thy law. At my own cost I will set up and maintain
a sufficient ministry, besides lecturers, in Mansoul.' This
obviously means the Established Church. Unable to
keep mankind directly in his own service, the Devil offers
to entangle them in the covenant of works, of which the
Church of England was the representative. Emmanuel
rebukes him for his guile and deceit. 'I will govern
Mansoul,' he says, 'by new laws, new officers, new motives, and new ways. I will pull down the town and
build it again, and it shall be as though it had not been,
and it shall be the glory of the whole universe.'

A second battle follows. Eargate is beaten in. The
Prince's army enters and advances as far as the old Recorder's house, where they knock and demand entrance.
'The old gentleman, not fully knowing their design, had
kept his gates shut all the time of the fight. He as yet
knew nothing of the great designs of Emmanuel, and
could not tell what to think.' The door is violently
broken open, and the house is made Emmanuel's head-
quarters. The townspeople, with Conscience and Understanding at their head, petition that their lives may be
spared; but Emmanuel gives no answer, Captain Boanerges
and Captain Conviction carrying terror into all hearts.
Diabolus, the cause of all the mischief, had retreated into
the castle.[1] He came out at last, and surrendered, and
in dramatic fitness he clearly ought now to have been
made away with in a complete manner. Unfortunately,
this could not be done. He was stripped of his armour,
bound to Emmanuel's chariot wheels, and thus turned
out of Mansoul 'into parched places in a salt land, where

[1] The heart.

he might seek rest and find none.' The salt land proved
as insecure a prison for this embarrassing being as the
pit where he was to have abode for ever.

Meanwhile, Mansoul being brought upon its knees,
the inhabitants were summoned into the castle yard,
when Conscience, Understanding, and Will be Will were
committed to ward. They and the rest again prayed
for mercy, but again without effect. Emmanuel was
silent. They drew another petition, and asked Captain
Conviction to present it for them. Captain Conviction
declined to be an advocate for rebels, and advised them to
send it by one of themselves, with a rope about his neck.
Mr. Desires Awake went with it. The Prince took it
from his hands, and wept as Desires Awake gave it in.
Emmanuel bade him go his way till the request could
be considered. The unhappy criminals knew not how to
take the answer. Mr. Understanding thought it promised
well. Conscience and Will be Will, borne down by shame
for their sins, looked for nothing but immediate death.
They tried again. They threw themselves on Emmanuel's
mercy. They drew up a confession of their horrible
iniquities. This, at least, they wished to offer to him
whether he would pity them or not. For a messenger
some of them thought of choosing one Old Good Deed.
Conscience, however, said that would never do. Emmanuel would answer, 'Is Old Good Deed yet alive in
Mansoul ? Then let Old Good Deed save it.' Desires
Awake went again with the rope on his neck, as Captain
Conviction recommended. Mr. Wet Eyes went with him,
wringing his hands.

Emmanuel still held out no comfort ; he promised
merely that in the camp the next morning he would give
such an answer as should be to his glory. Nothing but

the worst was now looked for. Mansoul passed the night
in sackcloth and ashes. When day broke, the prisoners
dressed themselves in mourning, and were carried to the
camp in chains, with ropes on their necks, beating their
breasts. Prostrate before Emmanuel's throne, they repeated their confession. They acknowledged that death
and the bottomless pit would be no more than a just retribution for their crimes. As they excused nothing and
promised nothing, Emmanuel at once delivered them
their pardons sealed with seven seals. He took off their
ropes and mourning, clothed them in shining garments,
and gave them chains and jewels.

Lord Will be Will 'swooned outright.' When he
recovered, 'the Prince' embraced and kissed him. The
bells in Mansoul were set ringing. Bonfires blazed. Emmanuel reviewed his army; and Mansoul, ravished at the
sight, prayed him to remain and be their King for ever.
He entered the city again in triumph, the people strewing
boughs and flowers before him. The streets and squares
were rebuilt on a new model. Lord Will be Will, now
regenerate, resumed the charge of the gates. The old
Lord Mayor was reinstated. Mr. Knowledge was made
Recorder, 'not out of contempt for old Conscience, who
was by-and-bye to have another employment.' Diabolus's
image was taken down and broken to pieces, and the
inhabitants of Mansoul were so happy that they sang of
Emmanuel in their sleep.

Justice, however, remained to be done on the hardened
and impenitent.

There were 'perhaps necessities in the nature of
things,' as Bishop Butler says, and an example could not
be made of the principal offender. But his servants and
old officials were lurking in the lanes and alleys. They

were apprehended, thrown into gaol, and brought to formal trial. Here we have Bunyan at his best. The scene in the court rises to the level of the famous trial of Faithful in Vanity Fair. The prisoners were Diabolus's Aldermen, Mr. Atheism, Mr. Incredulity, Mr. Lustings, Mr. Forget Good, Mr. Hardheart, Mr. Falsepeace, and the rest. The proceedings were precisely what Bunyan must have witnessed at a common English Assizes. The Judges were the new Recorder and the new Mayor. Mr. Do-right was Town Clerk. A jury was empanelled in the usual way. Mr. Knowall, Mr. Telltrue, and Mr. Hatelies were the principal witnesses.

Atheism was first brought to the bar, being charged 'with having pertinaciously and doltingly taught that there was no God.' He pleaded Not Guilty. Mr. Knowall was placed in the witness-box and sworn.

'My Lord,' he said, 'I know the prisoner at the bar. I and he were once in Villains Lane together, and he at that time did briskly talk of diverse opinions. And then and there I heard him say that for his part he did believe that there was no God. "But," said he, " I can profess one and be religious too, if the company I am in and the circumstances of other things," said he, " shall put me upon it." '

Telltrue and Hatelies were next called.

Telltrue. My Lord, I was formerly a great companion of the prisoner's, for the which I now repent me; and I have often heard him say, and with very great stomach-fulness, that he believed there was neither God, Angel, nor Spirit.

Town Clerk. Where did you hear him say so?

Telltrue. In Blackmouth Lane and in Blasphemers Row, and in many other places besides.

Town Clerk. Have you much knowledge of him?

Telltrue. I know him to be a Diabolonian, the son of a Diabolonian, and a horrible man to deny a Deity. His father's

name was Never be Good, and he had more children than this
Atheism.

Town Clerk. Mr. Hatelies. Look upon the prisoner at the
bar. Do you know him?

Hatelies. My Lord, this Atheism is one of the vilest wretches
that ever I came near or had to do with in my life. I have
heard him say that there is no God. I have heard him say that
there is no world to come, no sin, nor punishment hereafter;
and, moreover, I have heard him say that it was as good to go
to a bad-house as to go to hear a sermon.

Town Clerk. Where did you hear him say these things?

Hatelies. In Drunkards Row, just at Rascal Lane's End, at a
house in which Mr. Impiety lived.

The next prisoner was Mr. Lustings, who said that he
was of high birth and 'used to pleasures and pastimes of
greatness.' He had always been allowed to follow his own
inclinations, and it seemed strange to him that he should
be called in question for things which not only he but
every man secretly or openly approved.

When the evidence had been heard against him he
admitted frankly its general correctness.

'I,' he said, 'was ever of opinion that the happiest life
that a man could live on earth was to keep himself back
from nothing that he desired; nor have I been false at
any time to this opinion of mine, but have lived in the
love of my notions all my days. Nor was I ever so
churlish, having found such sweetness in them myself, as
to keep the commendation of them from others.'

Then came Mr. Incredulity. He was charged with
having encouraged the town of Mansoul to resist Shaddai.
Incredulity too had the courage of his opinions.

'I know not Shaddai,' he said. 'I love my old Prince.
I thought it my duty to be true to my trust, and to do
what I could to possess the minds of the men of Mansoul
to do their utmost to resist strangers and foreigners, and

with might to fight against them. Nor have I nor shall I change my opinion for fear of trouble, though you at present are possessed of place and power.'

Forget Good pleaded age and craziness. He was the son of a Diabolonian called Love Naught. He had uttered blasphemous speeches in Allbase Lane, next door to the sign of 'Conscience Seared with a Hot Iron;' also in Flesh Lane, right opposite the Church; also in Nauseous Street; also at the sign of the 'Reprobate,' next door to the 'Descent into the Pit.'

Falsepeace insisted that he was wrongly named in the indictment. His real name was Peace, and he had always laboured for peace. When war broke out between Shaddai and Diabolus, he had endeavoured to reconcile them, &c. Evidence was given that Falsepeace was his right designation. His father's name was Flatter. His mother, before she married Flatter, was called Mrs. Sootheup. When her child was born she always spoke of him as Falsepeace. She would call him twenty times a day, my little Falsepeace, my pretty Falsepeace, my sweet rogue Falsepeace! &c.

The court rejected his plea. He was told 'that he had wickedly maintained the town of Mansoul in rebellion against its king, in a false, lying, and damnable peace, contrary to the law of Shaddai. Peace that was not a companion of truth and holiness, was an accursed and treacherous peace, and was grounded on a lie.'

No Truth had assisted with his own hands in pulling down the image of Shaddai. He had set up the horned image of the beast Diabolus at the same place, and had torn and consumed all that remained of the laws of the king.

Pitiless said his name was not Pitiless, but Cheer

Up. He disliked to see Mansoul inclined to melancholy,
and that was all his offence. Pitiless, however, was
proved to be the name of him. It was a habit of the
Diabolonians to assume counterfeit appellations. Cove-
tousness called himself Good Husbandry; Pride called
himself Handsome; and so on.

Mr. Haughty's figure is admirably drawn in a few
lines. Mr. Haughty, when arraigned, declared 'that he
had carried himself bravely, not considering who was
his foe, or what was the cause in which he was engaged.
It was enough for him if he fought like a man and came
off victorious.'

The jury, it seems, made no distinctions between
opinions and acts. They did not hold that there was
any divine right in man to think what he pleased, and
to say what he thought. Bunyan had suffered as a martyr ;
but it was as a martyr for truth, not for general licence.
The genuine Protestants never denied that it was right
to prohibit men from teaching lies, and to punish them
if they disobeyed. The persecution of which they complained was the persecution of the honest man by the
knave.

All the prisoners were found guilty by a unanimous
verdict. Even Mr. Moderate, who was one of the jury,
thought a man must be wilfully blind who wished to
spare them. They were sentenced to be executed the
next day. Incredulity contrived to escape in the night.
Search was made for him, but he was not to be found in
Mansoul. He had fled beyond the walls, and had joined
Diabolus near Hell Gate. The rest, we are told, were
crucified—crucified by the hands of the men of Mansoul
themselves. They fought and struggled at the place of
execution so violently that Shaddai's secretary was obliged

to send assistance. But justice was done at last, and all
the Diabolonians, except Incredulity, were thus made an
end of.

They were made an end of for a time only. Mansoul,
by faith in Christ, and by the help of the Holy Spirit,
had crucified all manner of sin in its members. It was
faith that had now the victory. Unbelief had, unfortunately, escaped. It had left Mansoul for the time,
and had gone to its master the Devil. But unbelief,
being intellectual, had not been crucified with the sins of
the flesh, and thus could come back, and undo the work
which faith had accomplished. I do not know how far
this view approves itself to the more curious theologians.
Unbelief itself is said to be a product of the will; but an
allegory must not be cross-questioned too minutely.

The cornucopia of spiritual blessings was now opened
on Mansoul. All offences were fully and completely forgiven. A Holy Law and Testament was bestowed on
the people for their comfort and consolation, with a portion of the grace which dwelt in the hearts of Shaddai
and Emmanuel themselves. They were to be allowed
free access to Emmanuel's palace at all seasons, he himself
undertaking to hear them and redress their grievances,
and they were empowered and enjoined to destroy all
Diabolonians who might be found at any time within
their precincts.

These grants were embodied in a charter which was
set up in gold letters on the castle door. Two ministers
were appointed to carry on the government—one from
Shaddai's court; the other a native of Mansoul. The
first was Shaddai's chief secretary, the Holy Spirit. He,
if they were obedient and well-conducted, would be ' ten
times better to them than the whole world.' But they

were cautioned to be careful of their behaviour, for if they grieved him he would turn against them, and the worst might then be looked for. The second minister was the old Recorder, Mr. Conscience, for whom, as was said, a new office had been provided. The address of Emmanuel to Conscience in handing his commission to him contains the essence of Bunyan's creed.

'Thou must confine thyself to the teaching of moral virtues, to civil and natural duties. But thou must not attempt to presume to be a revealer of those high and supernatural mysteries that are kept close in the bosom of Shaddai, my father. For those things knows no man ; nor can any reveal them but my father's secretary only. . . . In all high and supernatural things, thou must go to him for information and knowledge. Wherefore keep low and be humble ; and remember that the Diabolonians that kept not their first charge, but left their own standing, are now made prisoners in the pit. Be therefore content with thy station. I have made thee my father's vicegerent on earth in the things of which I have made mention before. Take thou power to teach them to Mansoul ; yea, to impose them with whips and chastisements if they shall not willingly hearken to do thy commandments. . . . And one thing more to my beloved Mr. Recorder, and to all the town of Mansoul. You must not dwell in nor stay upon anything of that which he hath in commission to teach you, as to your trust and expectation of the next world. Of the next world, I say ; for I purpose to give another to Mansoul when this is worn out. But for that you must wholly and solely have recourse to and make stay upon the doctrine of your teacher of the first order. Yea, Mr. Recorder himself must not look for life from that which he himself revealeth. His dependence for that must be founded in the doctrine of the other preacher. Let Mr. Recorder also take heed that he receive not any doctrine or points of doctrine that are not communicated to him by his superior teacher, nor yet within the precincts of his own formal knowledge.'

Here, as a work of art, the ' Holy War ' should have its natural end. Mansoul had been created pure and happy. The Devil plotted against it, took it, defiled it. The Lord of the town came to the rescue, drove the Devil out, executed his officers and destroyed his works. Mansoul, according to Emmanuel's promise, was put into a better condition than that in which it was originally placed. New laws was drawn for it. New ministers were appointed to execute them. Vice had been destroyed. Unbelief had been driven away. The future lay serene and bright before it; all trials and dangers being safely passed. Thus we have all the parts of a complete drama—the fair beginning, the perils, the struggles, and the final victory of good. At this point, for purposes of art, the curtain ought to fall.

For purposes of art—not, however, for purposes of truth. For the drama of Mansoul was still incomplete, and will remain incomplete till man puts on another nature or ceases altogether to be. Christianity might place him in a new relation to his Maker, and, according to Bunyan, might expel the Devil out of his heart. But for practical purposes, as Mansoul too well knows, the Devil is still in possession. At intervals—as in the first centuries of the Christian era, for a period in the middle ages, and again in Protestant countries for another period at the Reformation—mankind made noble efforts to drive him out, and make the law of God into reality. But he comes back again, and the world is again as it was. The

vices again flourish which had been nailed to the Cross.
The statesman finds it as little possible as ever to take
moral right and justice for his rule in politics. The
Evangelical preacher continues to confess and deplore
the desperate wickedness of the human heart. The Devil
had been deposed, but his faithful subjects have restored
him to his throne. The stone of Sisyphus has been brought
to the brow of the hill only to rebound again to the
bottom. The old battle has to be fought a second
time, and, for all we can see, no closing victory will ever
be in 'this country of Universe.' Bunyan knew this but
too well. He tries to conceal it from himself by treating
Mansoul alternately as the soul of a single individual
from which the Devil may be so expelled as never danger-
ously to come back, or as the collective souls of the Christian world. But, let him mean which of the two he will,
the overpowering fact remains that, from the point of view
of his own theology, the great majority of mankind are
the Devil's servants through life, and are made over to
him everlastingly when their lives are over; while the
human race itself continues to follow its idle amusements
and its sinful pleasures as if no Emmanuel had ever come
from heaven to rescue it. Thus the situation is incomplete, and the artistic treatment necessarily unsatisfactory
—nay in a sense even worse than unsatisfactory, for the
attention of the reader, being reawakened by the fresh and
lively treatment of the subject, refuses to be satisfied with
conventional explanatory commonplaces. His mind is
puzzled; his faith wavers in its dependence upon a Being
who can permit His work to be spoilt, His power defied,
His victories even, when won, made useless.

Thus we take up the continuation of the 'Holy War'
with a certain weariness and expectation of disappoint-

ment. The delivery of Mansoul has not been finished after all, and, for all that we can see, the struggle between Shaddai and Diabolus may go on to eternity. Emmanuel, before he withdraws his presence, warns the inhabitants that many Diabolonians are still lurking about the outside walls of the town.[1] The names are those in St. Paul's list —Fornication, Adultery, Murder, Anger, Lasciviousness, Deceit, Evil Eye, Drunkenness, Revelling, Idolatry, Witchcraft, Variance, Emulation, Wrath, Strife, Sedition, Heresy. If all these were still abroad, not much had been gained by the crucifixion of the Aldermen. For the time, it was true, they did not show themselves openly. Mansoul after the conquest was clothed in white linen, and was in a state of peace and glory. But the linen was speedily soiled again. Mr. Carnal Security became a great person in Mansoul. The Chief Secretary's functions fell early into abeyance. He discovered the Recorder and Lord Will be Will at dinner in Mr. Carnal Security's parlour, and ceased to communicate with them. Mr. Godly Fear sounded an alarm, and Mr. Carnal Security's house was burnt by the mob ; but Mansoul's backslidings grew worse. It had its fits of repentance, and petitioned Emmanuel, but the messenger could have no admittance. The Lusts of the Flesh came out of their dens. They held a meeting in the room of Mr. Mischief, and wrote to invite Diabolus to return. Mr. Profane carried their letter to Hell Gate. Cerberus opened it, and a cry of joy ran through the prison. Beelzebub, Lucifer, Apollyon, and the rest of the devils came crowding to hear the news. Deadman's bell was rung. Diabolus addressed the assembly, putting them in hopes of recovering their prize. 'Nor need you fear, he said, that if ever we get Mansoul again, we after that

[1] The Flesh.

shall be cast out any more. It is the law of that Prince that now they own, that if we get them a second time they shall be ours for ever.' He returned a warm answer to his friend, ' which was subscribed as given at the Pit's mouth, by the joint consent of all the Princes of Darkness, by me, Diabolus.' The plan was to corrupt Mansoul's morals, and three devils of rank set off disguised to take service in the town, and make their way into the households of Mr. Mind, Mr. Godly Fear, and Lord Will be Will. Godly Fear discovered his mistake and turned the devil out. The other two established themselves successfully, and Mr. Profane was soon at Hell Gate again to report progress. Cerberus welcomed him with a ' St. Mary, I am glad to see thee.' Another council was held in Pandemonium, and Diabolus was impatient to show himself again on the scene. Apollyon advised him not to be in a hurry. ' Let our friends,' he said, ' draw Mansoul more and more into sin—there is nothing like sin to devour Mansoul ; ' but Diabolus would not wait for so slow a process, and raised an army of Doubters ' from the land of Doubting on the confines of Hell Gate Hill.' ' Doubt,' Bunyan always admitted, had been his own most dangerous enemy.

Happily the townspeople became aware of the peril which threatened them. Mr. Prywell, a great lover of Mansoul, overheard some Diabolonians talking about it at a place called Vile Hill. He carried his information to the Lord Mayor ; the Recorder rang the Alarm Bell ; Mansoul flew to penitence, held a day of fasting and humiliation, and prayed to Shaddai. The Diabolonians were hunted out, and all that could be found were killed. So far as haste and alarm would permit, Mansoul mended its ways. But on came the Doubting

army, led by Incredulity, who had escaped crucifixion—'none was truer to Diabolus than he'—on they
came under their several captains, Vocation Doubters,
Grace Doubters, Salvation Doubters, &c.—figures now
gone to shadow; then the deadliest foes of every English
Puritan soul. Mansoul appealed passionately to the Chief
Secretary; but the Chief Secretary 'had been grieved,'
and would have nothing to say to it. The town legions
went out to meet the invaders with good words, Prayer,
and singing of Psalms. The Doubters replied with
'horrible objections,' which were frightfully effective.
Lord Reason was wounded in the head and the Lord
Mayor in the eye; Mr. Mind received a shot in the sto-
mach, and Conscience was hit near the heart; but the
wounds were not mortal. Mansoul had the best of it in the
first engagement. Terror was followed by boasting and
self-confidence; a night sally was attempted—night being
the time when the Doubters were strongest. The sally
failed, and the men of Mansoul were turned to rout.
Diabolus's army attacked Eargate, stormed the walls,
forced their way into the town, and captured the whole
of it except the castle. Then 'Mansoul became a den of
dragons, an emblem of Hell, a place of total darkness.'
'Mr. Conscience's wounds so festered that he could have
no rest day or night.' 'Now a man might have walked
for days together in Mansoul, and scarce have seen one in
the town that looked like a religious man. Oh, the fearful state of Mansoul now!' 'Now every corner swarmed
with outlandish Doubters; Red Coats and Black Coats
walked the town by clusters, and filled the houses with
hideous noises, lying stories, and blasphemous language
against Shaddai and his Son.'

This is evidently meant for fashionable London in the

time of Charles II.   Bunyan was loyal to the King.   He
was no believer in moral regeneration through political
revolution.   But none the less he could see what was
under his eyes, and he knew what to think of it.

All was not lost, for the castle still held out.   The
only hope was in Emmanuel, and the garrison proposed to
petition again in spite of the ill reception of their first
messengers.   Godly Fear reminded them that no petition
would be received which was not signed by the Lord
Secretary, and that the Lord Secretary would sign nothing
which he had not himself drawn up.   The Lord Secretary,
when appealed to in the proper manner, no longer refused
his assistance.   Captain Credence flew up to Shaddai's
court with the simple words that Mansoul renounced all
trust in its own strength and relied upon its Saviour.
This time its prayer would be heard.

The devils meanwhile, triumphant though they were,
discovered that they could have no permanent victory
unless they could reduce the castle.   'Doubters at a
distance,' Beelzebub said, 'are but like objections repelled
by arguments.   Can we but get them into the hold, and
make them possessors of that, the day will be our own.'
The object was, therefore, to corrupt Mansoul at the
heart.

Then follows a very curious passage.   Bunyan had
still his eye on England, and had discerned the quarter
from which her real danger would approach.   Mansoul,
the Devil perceived, 'was a market town, much given to
commerce.'   'It would be possible to dispose of some of
the Devil's wares there.'   The people would be filled full,
and made rich, and would forget Emmanuel.   'Mansoul,'
they said, 'shall be so cumbered with abundance, that
they shall be forced to make their castle a warehouse.'

Wealth once made the first object of existence, 'Diabolus's gang will have easy entrance, and the castle will be our own.'

Political economy was still sleeping in the womb of futurity. Diabolus was unable to hasten its birth, and an experiment which Bunyan thought would certainly have succeeded was not to be tried. The *Deus ex Machinâ* appeared with its flaming sword. The Doubting army was cut to pieces, and Mansoul was saved. Again, however, the work was imperfectly done. Diabolus, like the bad genius in the fairy tale, survived for fresh mischief. Diabolus flew off again to Hell Gate, and was soon at the head of a new host; part composed of fugitive Doubters whom he rallied, and part of a new set of enemies called *Bloodmen*, by whom we are to understand persecutors, 'a people from a land that lay under the Dog Star.' 'Captain Pope' was chief of the Bloodmen. His escutcheon 'was the stake, the flame, and good men in it.' The Bloodmen had done Diabolus wonderful service in time past. 'Once they had forced Emmanuel out of the Kingdom of the Universe, and why, thought he, might they not do it again?'

Emmanuel did not this time go in person to the encounter. It was enough to send his captains. The Doubters fled at the first onset. 'The Bloodmen, when they saw that no Emmanuel was in the field, concluded that no Emmanuel was in Mansoul. Wherefore, they, looking upon what the captains did to be, as they called it, a fruit of the extravagancy of their wild and foolish fancies, rather despised them than feared them.' 'They proved, nevertheless, chicken-hearted, when they saw themselves matched and equalled.' The chiefs were taken prisoners, and brought to trial like Atheism and his

companions, and so, with an address from the Prince, the
story comes to a close.

Thus at last the 'Holy War' ends or seems to end.
It is as if Bunyan had wished to show that though the
converted Christian was still liable to the assaults of
Satan, and even to be beaten down and overcome by
him, his state was never afterwards so desperate as it
had been before the redemption, and that he had assistance ready at hand to save him when near extremity.
But the reader whose desire it is that good shall triumph
and evil be put to shame and overthrown remains
but partially satisfied; and the last conflict and its issues
leave Mansoul still subject to fresh attacks. Diabolus
was still at large. Carnal Sense broke prison and continued to lurk in the town. Unbelief 'was a nimble
Jack: him they could never lay hold of, though they
attempted to do it often.' Unbelief remained in Mansoul till the time that Mansoul ceased to dwell in the
country of the Universe; and where Unbelief was Diabolus would not be without a friend to open the gates
to him. Bunyan says, indeed, that 'he was stoned as
often as he showed himself in the streets.' He shows
himself in the streets much at his ease in these days of
ours after two more centuries.

Here lies the real weakness of the 'Holy War.' It
may be looked at either as the war in the soul of each
sinner that is saved, or as the war for the deliverance of
humanity. Under the first aspect it leaves out of sight
the large majority of mankind who are not supposed to
be saved, and out of whom, therefore, Diabolus is not
driven at all. Under the other aspect the struggle is
still unfinished; the last act of the drama has still to be
played, and we know not what the conclusion is to be.

To attempt to represent it, therefore, as a work of art,
with a beginning, a middle, and an end, is necessarily a
failure. The mysteries and contradictions which the
Christian revelation leaves unsolved are made tolerable to
us by Hope. We are prepared to find in religion many
things which we cannot understand; and difficulties do
not perplex us so long as they remain in a form to which
we are accustomed. To emphasise the problem by offering
it to us in an allegory, of which we are presumed to possess
a key, serves only to revive Man Friday's question, or
the old dilemma which neither intellect nor imagination
has ever dealt with successfully. 'Deus aut non vult
tollere mala, aut nequit. Si non vult non est bonus. Si
nequit non est omnipotens.' It is wiser to confess with
Butler that 'there may be necessities in the nature of
things which we are not acquainted with.'

CHAPTER IX.

THE PILGRIM'S PROGRESS.

If the 'Holy War' is an unfit subject for allegorical treatment, the 'Pilgrim's Progress' is no less perfectly adapted for it. The 'Holy War' is a representation of the struggle of human nature with evil, and the struggle is left undecided. The 'Pilgrim's Progress' is a representation of the efforts of a single soul after holiness, which has its natural termination when the soul quits its mortal home and crosses the dark river. Each one of us has his own life battle to fight out, his own sorrows and trials, his own failures or successes, and his own end. He wins the game, or he loses it. The account is wound up, and the curtain falls upon him. Here Bunyan had a material as excellent in itself as it was exactly suited to his peculiar genius; and his treatment of the subject from his own point of view—that of English Protestant Christianity—is unequalled and never will be equalled. I may say never, for in this world of change the point of view alters fast, and never continues in one stay. As we are swept along the stream of time, lights and shadows shift their places, mountain plateaus turn to sharp peaks, mountain ranges dissolve into vapour. The river which has been gliding deep and slow along the plain, leaps suddenly over a precipice and plunges foaming down a sunless gorge. In the midst of changing circumstances the central question remains the same—What am I ? what is this world in which I appear and disappear like a bubble ? who made me ? and what am I to do ? Some answer or other the mind of man demands and insists on receiving. Theologian or poet offers at long intervals explanations which are accepted as credible for a time. They wear out, and another follows, and then another. Bunyan's answer has served average English men and women for two hundred years, but no human being with Bunyan's intellect and Bunyan's sincerity can again use similar language; and the ' Pilgrim's Progress ' is and will re- main unique of its kind—an imperishable monument of the form in which the problem presented itself to a per- son of singular truthfulness, simplicity, and piety, who after many struggles accepted the Puritan creed as the adequate solution of it. It was composed exactly at the time when it was possible for such a book to come into being ; the close of the period when the Puritan formula was a real belief, and was about to change from a living principle into an intellectual opinion. So long as a re- ligion is fully alive, men do not talk about it or make allegories about it. They assume its truth as out of reach of question, and they simply obey its precepts as they obey the law of the land. It becomes a subject of art and discourse only when men are unconsciously ceasing to believe, and therefore the more vehemently think that they believe, and repudiate with indignation the sugges- tion that doubt has found its way into them. After this religion no longer governs their lives. It governs only the language in which they express themselves, and they preserve it eagerly, in the shape of elaborate observances or in the agreeable forms of art and literature.

The 'Pilgrim's Progress' was written before the 'Holy War,' while Bunyan was still in prison at Bedford, and was but half conscious of the gifts which he possessed. It was written for his own entertainment, and therefore without the thought—so fatal in its effects and so hard to be resisted—of what the world would say about it. It was written in compulsory quiet, when he was comparatively unexcited by the effort of perpetual preaching, and the shapes of things could present themselves to him as they really were, undistorted by theological narrowness. It is the same story which he has told of himself in 'Grace Abounding,' thrown out into an objective form.

He tells us himself, in a metrical introduction, the circumstances under which it was composed :—

> When at the first I took my pen in hand,
> Thus for to write, I did not understand
> That I at all should make a little book
> In such a mode. Nay, I had undertook
> To make another, which when almost done,
> Before I was aware I this begun.

> And thus it was.—I writing of the way
> And race of saints in this our Gospel day,
> Fell suddenly into an Allegory
> About the journey and the way to glory
> In more than twenty things which I set down.
> This done, I twenty more had in my crown,
> And these again began to multiply,
> Like sparks that from the coals of fire do fly.
> Nay then, thought I, if that you breed so fast
> I'll put you by yourselves, lest you at last
> Should prove *ad Infinitum*, and eat out
> The book that I already am about.

> Well, so I did ; but yet I did not think
> To show to all the world my pen and ink

In such a mode.   I only thought to make,
I knew not what.   Nor did I undertake
Merely to please my neighbours; no, not I.
I did it mine own self to gratify.

Neither did I but vacant seasons spend
In this my scribble; nor did I intend
But to divert myself in doing this
From worser thoughts which make me do amiss.
Thus I set pen to paper with delight,
And quickly had my thoughts in black and white;
For having now my method by the end,
Still as I pulled it came; and so I penned
It down: until at last it came to be
For length and breadth the bigness which you see.

Well, when I had thus put my ends together,
I showed them others, that I might see whether
They would condemn them or them justify.
And some said, Let them live; some, Let them die;
Some said, John, print it; others said, Not so;
Some said it might do good; others said, No.

Now was I in a strait, and did not see
Which was the best thing to be done by me.
At last I thought, since you are thus divided,
I print it will; and so the case decided.

The difference of opinion among Bunyan's friends is
easily explicable.   The allegoric representation of religion
to men profoundly convinced of the truth of it might
naturally seem light and fantastic, and the breadth of
the conception could not please the narrow sectarians
who knew no salvation beyond the lines of their peculiar
formulas.   The Pilgrim though in a Puritan dress is a
genuine man.   His experience is so truly human experience, that Christians of every persuasion can identify
themselves with him; and even those who regard
Christianity itself as but a natural outgrowth of the

conscience and intellect, and yet desire to live nobly and make the best of themselves, can recognise familiar foot-prints in every step of Christian's journey. Thus the 'Pilgrim's Progress' is a book, which, when once read, can never be forgotten. We too, every one of us, are pilgrims on the same road, and images and illustrations come back upon us from so faithful an itinerary, as we encounter similar trials, and learn for ourselves the accuracy with which Bunyan has described them. There is no occasion to follow a story minutely which memory can so universally supply. I need pause only at a few spots which are too charming to pass by.

How picturesque and vivid are the opening lines:

'As I walked through the wilderness of this world I lighted on a certain place where there was a den,[1] and I laid me down in that place to sleep, and as I slept I dreamed a dream. I dreamed, and behold I saw a man, a man clothed in rags, standing with his face from his own home with a book in his hand, and a great burden upon his back.'

The man is Bunyan himself as we see him in 'Grace Abounding.' His sins are the burden upon his back. He reads his book and weeps and trembles. He speaks of his fears to his friends and kindred. They think 'some frenzy distemper has got into his head.' He meets a man in the fields whose name is Evangelist. Evangelist tells him to flee from the City of Destruction. He shows him the way by which he must go, and points to the far-off light which will guide him to the wicket-gate. He sets off, and his neighbours of course think him mad. The world always thinks men mad who turn their backs upon it. Obstinate and Pliable (how well we know them

---

[1] The Bedford Prison.

both !) follow to persuade him to return.   Obstinate talks
practical common sense to him, and as it has no effect,
gives him up as a fantastical fellow.   Pliable thinks that
there may be something in what he says, and offers to go
with him.

Before they can reach the wicket-gate, they fall into
a 'miry slough.'   Who does not know the miry slough
too ?   When a man begins for the first time to think
seriously about himself, the first thing that rises before
him is a consciousness of his miserable past life.   Amendment seems to be desperate.   He thinks it is too late to
change for any useful purpose, and he sinks into despondency.

Pliable finding the road disagreeable has soon had
enough of it.   He scrambles out of the slough 'on the
side which was nearest to his own house' and goes home.
Christian struggling manfully is lifted out 'by a man
whose name was Help,' and goes on upon his journey,
but the burden on his back weighs him down.   He falls
in with Mr. Worldly Wiseman who lives in the town
of Carnal Policy.   Mr. Worldly Wiseman, who looks like
a gentleman, advises him not to think about his sins.
If he has done wrong he must alter his life and do
better for the future.   He directs him to a village called
Morality, where he will find a gentleman well known in
those parts, who will take his burden off—Mr. Legality.
Either Mr. Legality will do it himself, or it can be done
equally well by his pretty young son, Mr. Civility.

The way to a better life does not lie in a change of
outward action, but in a changed heart.   Legality soon
passes into civility, according to the saying that vice loses
half its evil when it loses its grossness.   Bunyan would
have said that the poison was the more deadly from being

concealed.   Christian after a near escape is set straight
again.   He is admitted into the wicket-gate and is directed
how he is to go forward.   He asks if he may not lose his
way.   He is answered Yes, 'There are many ways (that)
butt down on this and they are crooked and wide.   But
thus thou mayest know the right from the wrong, that
only being straight and narrow.'

Good people often suppose that when a man is once
'converted,' as they call it, and has entered on a religious
life, he will find everything made easy.   He has turned
to Christ, and in Christ he will find rest and pleasantness.
The path of duty is unfortunately not strewed with
flowers at all.   The primrose road leads to the other
place.   As on all other journeys, to persevere is the
difficulty.   The pilgrim's feet grow sorer the longer he
walks.   His lower nature follows him like a shadow
watching opportunities to trip him up, and ever appear-
ing in some new disguise.   In the way of comfort he
is allowed only certain resting places, quiet intervals of
peace when temptation is absent, and the mind can gather
strength and encouragement from a sense of the progress
which it has made.

The first of these resting places at which Christian
arrives is the 'Interpreter's House.'   This means, I conceive, that he arrives at a right understanding of the
objects of human desire as they really are.   He learns to
distinguish there between passion and patience, passion
which demands immediate gratification, and patience
which can wait and hope.   He sees the action of grace
on the heart, and sees the Devil labouring to put it out.
He sees the man in the iron cage who was once a flourish-
ing professor, but had been tempted away by pleasure and
had sinned against light.   He hears a dream too—one of

Bunyan's own early dreams, but related as by another
person. The Pilgrim himself was beyond the reach of
such uneasy visions. But it shows how profoundly the
terrible side of Christianity had seized on Bunyan's imagination and how little he was able to forget it.

'This night as I was in my sleep I dreamed, and
behold the heavens grew exceeding black : also it thun-
dered and lightened in most fearful wise, that it put me
into an agony ; so I looked up in my dream and saw the
clouds rack at an unusual rate, upon which I heard a
great sound of a trumpet, and saw also a man sit upon a
cloud attended with the thousands of heaven. They
were all in a flaming fire, and the heaven also was in a
burning flame. I heard then a voice, saying, Arise ye
dead and come to judgment; and with that the rocks
rent, the graves opened, and the dead that were therein
came forth. Some of them were exceeding glad and
looked upward, some sought to hide themselves under the
mountains. Then I saw the man that sate upon the
cloud open the book and bid the world draw near. Yet
there was, by reason of a fierce flame that issued out and
came from before him, a convenient distance betwixt
him and them, as betwixt the judge and the prisoners at
the bar. I heard it also proclaimed to them that attended
on the man that sate on the cloud, Gather together the
tares, the chaff, and the stubble, and cast them into the
burning lake. And with that the bottomless pit opened
just whereabouts I stood, out of the mouth of which
there came in an abundant manner smoke and coals of
fire with hideous noises. It was also said to the same
persons, Gather the wheat into my garner. And with
that I saw many catched up and carried away into the
clouds, but I was left behind. I also sought to hide

myself, but I could not, for the man that sate upon the
cloud still kept his eye upon me. My sins also came into
my mind, and my conscience did accuse me on every
side. I thought the day of judgment was come and I
was not ready for it.'

The resting time comes to an end. The Pilgrim
gathers himself together, and proceeds upon his way.
He is not to be burdened for ever with the sense of his
sins. It fell from off his back at the sight of the cross.
Three shining ones appear and tell him that his sins are
forgiven ; they take off his rags and provide him with a
new suit.

He now encounters fellow-travellers ; and the seriousness of the story is relieved by adventures and humorous
conversations. At the bottom of a hill he finds three
gentlemen asleep, ' a little out of the way.' These were
Simple, Sloth, and Presumption. He tries to rouse
them, but does not succeed. Presently two others are
seen tumbling over the wall into the Narrow Way. They
are come from the land of Vain Glory, and are called
Formalist and Hypocrisy. Like the Pilgrim, they are
bound for Mount Zion ; but the wicket-gate was ' too far
about,' and they had come by a short cut. ' They had
custom for it a thousand years and more ; and custom
being of so long standing would be admitted legal by any
impartial judge.' Whether right or wrong they insist
that they are in the way, and no more is to be said.
But they are soon out of it again. The hill is the hill
Difficulty, and the road parts into three. Two go round
the bottom, as modern engineers would make them. The
other rises straight over the top. Formalist and Hypocrisy choose the easy ways, and are heard of no more.
Pilgrim climbs up, and after various accidents comes to

the second resting-place, the Palace Beautiful, built by
the Lord of the Hill to entertain strangers in. The re-
collections of Sir Bevis of Southampton furnished Bunyan
with his framework. Lions guard the court. Fair ladies
entertain him as if he had been a knight-errant in quest
of the Holy Grail. The ladies, of course, are all that they
ought to be: the Christian graces—Discretion, Prudence,
Piety, and Charity. He tells them his history. They ask
him if he has brought none of his old belongings with
him. He answers yes; but greatly against his will: his
inward and carnal cogitations, with which his countrymen, as well as himself, were so much delighted. Only in
golden hours they seemed to leave him. Who cannot
recognise the truth of this? Who has not groaned over
the follies and idiotcies that cling to us like the doggerel
verses that hang about our memories? The room in
which he sleeps is called Peace. In the morning he is
shown the curiosities, chiefly Scripture relics, in the
palace. He is taken to the roof, from which he sees far
off the outlines of the Delectable Mountains. Next, the
ladies carry him to the armoury, and equip him for the
dangers which lie next before him. He is to go down
into the Valley of Humiliation, and pass thence through
the Valley of the Shadow of Death.

Bunyan here shows the finest insight. To some pilgrims the Valley of Humiliation was the pleasantest part
of the journey. Mr. Feeblemind, in the second part of
the story, was happier there than anywhere. But Christian is Bunyan himself; and Bunyan had a stiff self-
willed nature, and had found his spirit the most stubborn
part of him. Down here he encounters Apollyon himself, 'straddling quite over the whole breadth of the way'—
a more effective devil than the Diabolus of the 'Holy

War.' He fights him for half-a-day, is sorely wounded
in head, hand, and foot, and has a near escape of being
pressed to death.   Apollyon spreads his bat wings at last,
and flies away; but there remains the Valley of the
Shadow of Death, the dark scene of lonely horrors.
Two men meet him on the borders of it.   They tell him
the valley is full of spectres; and they warn him, if he
values his life, to go back.   Well Bunyan knew these
spectres, those dreary misgivings that he was toiling after
an illusion; that 'good' and 'evil' had no meaning except
on earth, and for man's convenience ; and that he himself
was but a creature of a day, allowed a brief season of
what is called existence, and then to pass away and be
as if he had never been.   It speaks well for Bunyan's
honesty that this state of mind which religious people
generally call wicked is placed directly in his Pilgrim's
path, and he is compelled to pass through it.   In the
valley, close at the road-side, there is a pit, which is one
of the mouths of hell.   A wicked spirit whispers to him
as he goes by.   He imagines that the thought had pro-
ceeded out of his own heart.

    The sky clears when he is beyond the gorge.   Outside
it are the caves where the two giants, Pope and Pagan,
had lived in old times.   Pagan had been dead many a
day.   Pope was still living, 'but he had grown so crazy
and stiff in his joints that he could now do little more
than sit in his cave's mouth, grinning at pilgrims as they
went by, and biting his nails because he could not come
at them.'

    Here he overtakes 'Faithful,' a true pilgrim like him-
self.   Faithful had met with trials; but his trials have
not resembled Christian's.   Christian's difficulties, like
Bunyan's own, had been all spiritual.   'The lusts of the

flesh' seem to have had no attraction for him. Faithful
had been assailed by 'Wanton,' and had been obliged to
fly from her. He had not fallen into the slough; but he
had been beguiled by the Old Adam, who offered him one
of his daughters for a wife. In the Valley of the Shadow
of Death he had found sunshine all the way. Doubts
about the truth of religion had never troubled the simpler
nature of the good Faithful.

Mr. Talkative is the next character introduced, and
is one of the best figures which Bunyan has drawn; Mr.
Talkative, with Scripture at his fingers' ends, and perfect
master of all doctrinal subtleties, ready 'to talk of things
heavenly or things earthly, things moral or things evangelical, things sacred or things profane, things past or
things to come, things foreign or things at home, things
essential or things circumstantial, provided that all be
done to our profit.'

This gentleman would have taken in Faithful, who
was awed by such a rush of volubility. Christian has
seen him before, knows him well, and can describe him.
'He is the son of one Saywell. He dwelt in Prating
Row. He is for any company and for any talk. As he
talks now with you so will he talk when on the ale-
bench. The more drink he hath in his crown, the more
of these things he hath in his mouth. Religion hath no
place in his heart, or home, or conversation; all that he
hath lieth in his tongue, and his religion is to make a
noise therewith.'

The elect, though they have ceased to be of the world,
are still in the world. They are still part of the general
community of mankind, and share, whether they like it
or not, in the ordinary activities of life. Faithful and
Christian have left the City of Destruction. They have

shaken off from themselves all liking for idle pleasures. They nevertheless find themselves in their journey at Vanity Fair, 'a fair set up by Beelzebub 5000 years ago.' Trade of all sorts went on at Vanity Fair, and people of all sorts were collected there : cheats, fools, asses, knaves, and rogues. Some were honest, many were dishonest; some lived peaceably and uprightly, others robbed, murdered, seduced their neighbours' wives, or lied and perjured themselves. Vanity Fair was European society as it existed in the days of Charles II. Each nation was represented. There was British Row, French Row, and Spanish Row. 'The wares of Rome and her merchandise were greatly promoted at the fair, only the English nation with some others had taken a dislike to them.' The pilgrims appear on the scene as the Apostles appeared at Antioch and Rome, to tell the people that there were things in the world of more consequence than money and pleasure. The better sort listen. Public opinion in general calls them fools and Bedlamites. The fair becomes excited, disturbances are feared, and the authorities send to make inquiries. Authorities naturally disapprove of novelties ; and Christian and Faithful are arrested, beaten, and put in the cage. Their friends insist that they have done no harm, that they are innocent strangers teaching only what will make men better instead of worse. A riot follows. The authorities determine to make an example of them, and the result is the ever-memorable trial of the two pilgrims. They are brought in irons before my Lord Hategood, charged with 'disturbing the trade of the town, creating divisions, and making converts to their opinions in contempt of the law of the Prince.'

Faithful begins with an admission which would have

made it difficult for Hategood to let him off, for he says
that the Prince they talked of, being Beelzebub, the
enemy of the Lord, he defied him and all his angels.
Three witnesses were then called : Envy, Superstition,
and Pickthank.

Envy says that Faithful regards neither prince nor
people, but does all he can to possess men with disloyal
notions, which he call principles of faith and holiness.

Superstition says that he knows little of him, but has
heard him say that ' our religion is naught, and such by
which no man can please God, from which saying his
Lordship well knows will follow that we are yet in our
sins, and finally shall be damned.'

Pickthank deposes that he has heard Faithful rail on
Beelzebub, and speak contemptuously of his honourable
friends my Lord Old Man, my Lord Carnal Delight,
my Lord Luxurious, my Lord Desire of Vain Glory, my
Lord Lechery, Sir Having Greedy, and the rest of the
nobility, besides which he has railed against his lordship
on the bench himself, calling him an ungodly villain.

The evidence was perfectly true, and the prisoner,
when called on for his defence, confirmed it. He says
(avoiding the terms in which he was said to rail and
the like) that ' the Prince of the town, with all the rabble-
ment of his attendants by this gentleman named, are
more fit for a being in hell than in this town or country.'

Lord Hategood has been supposed to have been drawn
from one or other of Charles II.'s judges, perhaps from
either Twisden or Chester, who had the conversation with
Bunyan's wife. But it is difficult to see how either one
or the other could have acted otherwise than they did.
Faithful might be quite right. Hell might be and probably was the proper place for Beelzebub, and for all persons

holding authority under him.   But as a matter of fact, a form of society did for some purpose or other exist, and had been permitted to exist for 5000 years, owning Beelzebub's sovereignty.   It must defend itself, or must cease to be, and it could not be expected to make no effort at self-preservation.   Faithful had come to Vanity Fair to make a revolution—a revolution extremely desirable, but one which it was unreasonable to expect the constituted authorities to allow to go forward.   It was not a case of false witness.   A prisoner who admits that he has taught the people that their Prince ought to be in hell, and has called the judge an ungodly villain, cannot complain if he is accused of preaching rebellion.

Lord Hategood charges the jury, and explains the law. 'There was an Act made,' he says, 'in the days of Pharaoh the Great, servant to our Prince, that lest those of a contrary religion should multiply and grow too strong for him, their males should be thrown into the river.   There was also an Act made in the days of Nebuchadnezzar the Great, that whoever would not fall down and worship his golden image should be thrown into a fiery furnace. There was also an Act made in the days of Darius that whoso for some time called upon any God but him should be cast into the lion's den.   Now the substance of these laws this rebel hath broken, not only in thought (which is not to be borne), but also in word and deed, which must, therefore, be intolerable.   For that of Pharaoh, his law was made upon a supposition to prevent mischief, no crime being yet apparent.   For the second and third you see his disputations against our religion, and for the treason he hath confessed he deserveth to die the death.'

'Then went the jury out, whose names were Mr. Blindman, Mr. Nogood, Mr. Malice, Mr. Lovelust, Mr.

Liveloose, Mr. Heady, Mr. Highmind, Mr. Enmity, Mr. Liar, Mr. Cruelty, Mr. Hatelight, and Mr. Implacable, who every one gave in his private verdict against him among themselves, and afterwards unanimously concluded to bring him in guilty before the judge. And first, Mr. Blindman, the foreman, said : I see clearly that this man is a heretic. Then said Mr. No Good, Away with such a fellow from the earth. Aye, said Mr. Malice, I hate the very looks of him. Then said Mr. Lovelust, I could never endure him. Nor I, said Mr. Liveloose, for he would always be condemning my way. Hang him, hang him, said Mr. Heady. A sorry scrub, said Mr. Highmind. My heart riseth against him, said Mr. Enmity. He is a rogue, said Mr. Liar. Hanging is too good for him, said Mr. Cruelty. Let us despatch him out of the way, said Mr. Hatelight. Then, said Mr. Implacable, might I have all the world given me, I could not be reconciled to him ; therefore, let us forthwith bring him in guilty of death.'

Abstract qualities of character were never clothed in more substantial flesh and blood than these jurymen. Spenser's knights in the 'Fairy Queen' are mere shadows to them. Faithful was, of course, condemned, scourged, buffeted, lanced in his feet with knives, stoned, stabbed, at last burned, and spared the pain of travelling further on the narrow road. A chariot and horses were waiting to bear him through the clouds, the nearest way to the Celestial Gate. Christian, who it seems had been remanded, contrives to escape. He is joined by Hopeful, a convert whom he has made in the town, and they pursue their journey in company. A second person is useful dramatically, and Hopeful takes Faithful's place. Leaving Vanity Fair, they are again on the Pilgrim's road. There they encounter Mr. Bye-ends. Bye-ends comes from the

town of Plain-Speech, where he has a large kindred,
My Lord Turnabout, my Lord Timeserver, Mr. Facing-
both-ways, Mr. Two Tongues, the parson of the parish.
Bye-ends himself was married to a daughter of Lady
Feignings. Bunyan's invention in such things was in-
exhaustible.

They have more trials of the old kind with which
Bunyan himself was so familiar. They cross the River
of Life and even drink at it, yet for all this and directly
after, they stray into Bye Path Meadow. They lose
themselves in the grounds of Doubting Castle, and are
seized upon by Giant Despair—still a prey to doubt—
still uncertain whether religion be not a dream, even after
they have fought with wild beasts in Vanity Fair and
have drunk of the water of life. Nowhere does Bunyan
show better how well he knew the heart of man. Christian even thinks of killing himself in the dungeons of
Doubting Castle. Hopeful cheers him up, they break
their prison, recover the road again, and arrive at the
Delectable Mountains in Emmanuel's own land. There it
might be thought the danger would be over, but it is not
so. Even in Emmanuel's Land there is a door in the
side of a hill which is a byeway to hell, and beyond
Emmanuel's Land is the country of conceit, a new and
special temptation for those who think that they are
near salvation. Here they encounter 'a brisk lad of the
neighbourhood,' needed soon after for a particular purpose, who is a good liver, prays devoutly, fasts regularly,
pays tithes punctually, and hopes that everyone will get
to heaven by the religion which he professes, provided he
fears God and tries to do his duty. The name of this
brisk lad is Ignorance. Leaving him, they are caught in
a net by Flatterer, and are smartly whipped by 'a shining

one,' who lets them out of it. False ideas and vanity lay them open once more to their most dangerous enemy. They meet a man coming towards them from the direction in which they are going. They tell him that they are on the way to Mount Zion. He laughs scornfully and answers :—

'There is no such place as you dream of in all the world. When I was at home in my own country, I heard as you now affirm, and from hearing I went out to see ; and have been seeking this city these twenty years, but I find no more of it than I did the first day I went out. I am going back again and will seek to refresh myself with things which I then cast away for hopes of that which I now see is not.'

Still uncertainty—even on the verge of eternity—strange, doubtless, and reprehensible to Right Reverend persons, who never 'cast away' anything; to whom a religious profession has been a highway to pleasure and preferment, who live in the comfortable assurance that as it has been in this life so it will be in the next. Only moral obliquity of the worst kind could admit a doubt about so excellent a religion as this. But Bunyan was not a Right Reverend. Christianity had brought him no palaces and large revenues, and a place among the great of the land. If Christianity was not true his whole life was folly and illusion, and the dread that it might be so clung to his belief like its shadow.

The way was still long. The pilgrims reach the Enchanted Ground and are drowsy and tired. Ignorance comes up with them again. He talks much about himself. He tells them of the good motives that come into his mind and comfort him as he walks. His heart tells him that he has left all for God and Heaven. His belief

and his life agree together, and he is humbly confident
that his hopes are well-founded. When they speak to
him of Salvation by Faith and Conviction by Sin, he cannot understand what they mean. As he leaves them they
are reminded of one Temporary, ' once a forward man
in religion.' Temporary dwelt in Graceless, ' a town
two miles from Honesty, next door to one Turnback.'
He ' was going on pilgrimage, but became acquainted
with one Save Self, and was never more heard of.'

    These figures all mean something. They correspond
in part to Bunyan's own recollection of his own trials.
Partly he is indulging his humour by describing others
who were more astray than he was. It was over at last :
the pilgrims arrive at the land of Beulah, the beautiful
sunset after the storms were all past. Doubting Castle
can be seen no more, and between them and their last
rest there remains only the deep river over which there is
no bridge, the river of Death. On the hill beyond the
waters glitter the towers and domes of the Celestial
City ; but through the river they must first pass, and they
find it deeper or shallower according to the strength of
their faith. They go through, Hopeful feeling the bottom
all along ; Christian still in character, not without some
horror, and frightened by hobgoblins. On the other
side they are received by angels, and are carried to their
final home, to live for ever in the Prince's presence. Then
follows the only passage which the present writer reads
with regret in this admirable book. It is given to the
self-righteous Ignorance who, doubtless, had been provoking with ' his good motives that comforted him as
he walked ;' but Bunyan's zeal might have been satisfied
by inflicting a lighter chastisement upon him. He comes
up to the river. He crosses without the difficulties which

attended Christian and Hopeful. 'It happened that
there was then at the place one Vain Hope, a Ferryman,
that with his boat' (some viaticum or priestly absolution)
'helped him over.' He ascends the hill, and approaches
the city, but no angels are in attendance, 'neither did
any man meet him with the least encouragement.'
Above the gate there was the verse written—'Blessed
are they that do His commandments that they may have
right to the Tree of Life, and may enter in through the
gate into the city.' Bunyan, who believed that no man
could keep the commandments, and had no right to anything but damnation, must have introduced the words
as if to mock the unhappy wretch who, after all, had
tried to keep the commandments as well as most people,
and was seeking admittance, with a conscience moderately
at ease. 'He was asked by the men that looked over the
gate—Whence come you and what would you have?' He
answered, 'I have eaten and drunk in the presence of the
King, and he has taught in our street.' Then they asked
him for his certificate, that they might go in and show
it to the king. So he fumbled in his bosom for one and
found none. Then said they, 'Have you none?' But
the man answered never a word. So they told the king
but he would not come down to see him, but commanded
the two shining ones that conducted Christian and
Hopeful to the city to go out and take Ignorance and
bind him hand and foot, and have him away. Then
they took him up and carried him through the air to the
door in the side of the hill, and put him in there. 'Then,'
so Bunyan ends, 'I saw that there was a way to Hell
even from the gates of Heaven, as well as from the City
of Destruction; so I awoke, and behold it was a dream!'
     Poor Ignorance! Hell—such a place as Bunyan

imagined Hell to be—was a hard fate for a miserable
mortal who had failed to comprehend the true conditions
of justification. We are not told that he was a vain
boaster. He could not have advanced so near to the
door of Heaven if he had not been really a decent man,
though vain and silly. Behold, it was a dream! The
dreams which come to us when sleep is deep on the soul
may be sent direct from some revealing power. When
we are near waking, the supernatural insight may be
refracted through human theory.

Charity will hope that the vision of Ignorance cast
bound into the mouth of Hell, when he was knocking
at the gate of Heaven, came through Homer's ivory
gate, and that Bunyan here was a mistaken interpreter
of the spiritual tradition. The fierce inferences of
Puritan theology are no longer credible to us; yet nobler
men than the Puritans are not to be found in all English
history. It will be well if the clearer sight which enables
us to detect their errors, enables us also to recognise their
excellence.

The second part of the 'Pilgrim's Progress,' like most
second parts, is but a feeble reverberation of the first. It
is comforting, no doubt, to know that Christian's wife and
children were not left to their fate in the City of Destruction. But Bunyan had given us all that he had to tell
about the journey, and we do not need a repetition of it.
Of course there are touches of genius. No writing of
Bunyan's could be wholly without it. But the rough
simplicity is gone, and instead of it there is a tone of
sentiment which is almost mawkish. Giants, dragons, and
angelic champions carry us into a spurious fairy land,
where the knight-errant is a preacher in disguise. Fair
ladies and love matches, however decorously chastened,

suit ill with the sternness of the mortal conflict between
the soul and sin. Christiana and her children are tole-
rated for the pilgrim's sake to whom they belong. Had
they appealed to our interest on their own merits, we
would have been contented to wish them well through
their difficulties, and to trouble ourselves no further
about them.

CHAPTER X.

LAST DAYS AND DEATH.

LITTLE remains to be told of Bunyan's concluding years. No friends preserved his letters. No diaries of his own survive to gratify curiosity. Men truly eminent think too meanly of themselves or their work to care much to be personally remembered. He lived for sixteen years after his release from the gaol, and those years were spent in the peaceful discharge of his congregational duties, in writing, in visiting the scattered members of the Baptist communion, or in preaching in the villages and woods. His outward circumstances were easy. He had a small but well-provided house in Bedford, into which he collected rare and valuable pieces of old furniture and plate, and other articles—presents, probably, from those who admired him. He visited London annually to preach in the Baptist churches. The 'Pilgrim's Progress' spread his fame over England, over Europe, and over the American settlements. It was translated into many languages; and so catholic was its spirit, that it was adapted with a few alterations for the use even of the Catholics themselves. He abstained, as he had done steadily throughout his life, from all interference with politics, and the Government in turn never again meddled with him. He even received offers of promotion to larger spheres of action which might have tempted a meaner nature. But he could never be induced to leave Bedford, and there he quietly stayed through changes of ministry, Popish plots, and Monmouth rebellions, while the terror of a restoration of Popery was bringing on the Revolution; careless of kings and cabinets, and confident that Giant Pope had lost his power for harm, and thenceforward could only bite his nails at the passing pilgrims. Once only, after the failure of the Exclusion Bill, he seems to have feared that violent measures might again be tried against him. It is even said that he was threatened with arrest, and it was on this occasion that he made over his property to his wife. The policy of James II., however, transparently treacherous though it was, for the time gave security to the Nonconformist congregations, and in the years which immediately preceded the final expulsion of the Stuarts, liberty of conscience was under fewer restrictions than it had been in the most rigorous days of the Reformation, or under the Long Parliament itself. Thus the anxiety passed away, and Bunyan was left undisturbed to finish his earthly work.

He was happy in his family. His blind child, for whom he had been so touchingly anxious, had died while he was in prison. His other children lived and did well; and his brave companion, who had spoken so stoutly for him to the judges, continued at his side. His health, it was said, had suffered from his confinement; but the only serious illness which we hear of, was an attack of 'sweating sickness,' which came upon him in 1687, and from which he never thoroughly recovered. He was then fifty-nine, and in the next year he died.

His end was characteristic. It was brought on by exposure when he was engaged in an act of charity. A

quarrel had broken out in a family at Reading with which
Bunyan had some acquaintance. A father had taken
offence at his son, and threatened to disinherit him.
Bunyan undertook a journey on horseback from Bedford
to Reading in the hope of reconciling them. He succeeded, but at the cost of his life. Returning by London
he was overtaken on the road by a storm of rain, and was
wetted through before he could find shelter. The chill,
falling on a constitution already weakened by illness,
brought on fever. He was able to reach the house of
Mr. Strudwick, one of his London friends; but he never
left his bed afterwards. In ten days he was dead. The
exact date is uncertain. It was towards the end of
August 1688, between two and three months before the
landing of King William. He was buried in Mr. Strudwick's vault in the Dissenters' burying-ground at Bunhill
Fields. His last words were 'Take me, for I come to
Thee.'

So ended, at the age of sixty, a man who, if his importance may be measured by the influence which he has
exerted over succeeding generations, must be counted
among the most extraordinary persons whom England has
produced. It has been the fashion to dwell on the disad-
vantages of his education, and to regret the carelessness
of nature which brought into existence a man of genius
in a tinker's hut at Elstow. Nature is less partial than
she appears, and all situations in life have their compen-
sations along with them.

Circumstances, I should say, qualified Bunyan perfectly
well for the work which he had to do. If he had gone
to school, as he said, with Aristotle and Plato; if he had
been broken in at a university and been turned into a
bishop; if he had been in any one of the learned pro-

fessions, he might easily have lost or might have never
known the secret of his powers.   He was born to be the
Poet-apostle of the English middle classes, imperfectly
educated like himself ; and, being one of themselves, he
had the key of their thoughts and feelings in his own heart.
Like nine out of ten of his countrymen, he came into the
world with no fortune but his industry.   He had to work
with his hands for his bread, and to advance by the side
of his neighbours along the road of common business.
His knowledge was scanty, though of rare quality.   He
knew his Bible probably by heart.   He had studied
history in Foxe's 'Martyrs,' but nowhere else that we
can trace.   The rest of his mental furniture was gathered
at first hand from his conscience, his life, and his occupa-
tions.   Thus every idea which he received falling into a
soil naturally fertile, sprouted up fresh, vigorous, and
original.   He confessed to have felt—(as a man of his
powers could hardly have failed to feel)—continued doubts
about the Bible and the reality of the Divine government.
It has been well said that when we look into the world
to find the image of God, it is as if we were to stand
before a looking-glass expecting to see ourselves reflected
there, and to see nothing.   Education scarcely improves
our perception in this respect ; and wider information,
wider acquaintance with the thoughts of other men in
other ages and countries, might as easily have increased
his difficulties as have assisted him in overcoming them.
He was not a man who could have contented himself with
compromises and half-convictions.   No force could have
subdued him into a decent Anglican divine—a 'Mr.
Two Tongues, parson of the parish.'   He was passionate
and thorough-going.   The authority of conscience presented itself to him only in the shape of religious obli-

gation. Religion once shaken into a 'perhaps,' would have had no existence to him ; and it is easy to conceive a university-bred Bunyan, an intellectual meteor, flaring uselessly across the sky and disappearing in smoke and nothingness.

Powerful temperaments are necessarily intense. Bunyan, born a tinker, had heard right and wrong preached to him in the name of the Christian creed. He concluded after a struggle that Christianity was true, and on that conviction he built himself up into what he was. It might have been the same perhaps with Burns had he been born a century before. Given Christianity as an unquestionably true account of the situation and future prospects of man, the feature of it most appalling to the imagination is that hell-fire—a torment exceeding the most horrible which fancy can conceive, and extending into eternity—awaits the enormous majority of the human race. The dreadful probability seized hold on the young Bunyan's mind. He shuddered at it when awake. In the visions of the night it came before him in the tremendous details of the dreadful reality. It became the governing thought in his nature.

Such a belief, if it does not drive a man to madness, will at least cure him of trifling. It will clear his mind of false sentiment, take the nonsense out of him, and enable him to resist vulgar temptation as nothing else will. The danger is that the mind may not bear the strain, that the belief itself may crack and leave nothing. Bunyan was hardly tried, but in him the belief did not crack. It spread over his character. It filled him first with terror ; then with a loathing of sin, which entailed so awful a penalty ; then, as his personal fears were allayed

N

by the recognition of Christ, it turned to tenderness and pity.

There was no fanaticism in Bunyan; nothing harsh or savage. His natural humour perhaps saved him. His few recorded sayings all refer to the one central question; but healthy seriousness often best expresses itself in playful quaintness. He was once going somewhere disguised as a waggoner. He was overtaken by a constable who had a warrant to arrest him. The constable asked him if he knew that devil of a fellow Bunyan. 'Know him!' Bunyan said. 'You might call him a devil if you knew him as well as I once did.'

A Cambridge student was trying to show him what a divine thing reason was—'reason, the chief glory of man which distinguished him from a beast,' &c., &c.

Bunyan growled out: 'Sin distinguishes man from beast. Is sin divine?'

He was extremely tolerant in his terms of Church membership. He offended the stricter part of his congregation by refusing even to make infant baptism a condition of exclusion. The only persons with whom he declined to communicate were those whose lives were openly immoral. His chief objection to the Church of England was the admission of the ungodly to the Sacraments. He hated party titles and quarrels upon trifles. He desired himself to be called a Christian or a Believer, or 'any name which was approved by the Holy Ghost.' Divisions, he said, were to Churches like wars to countries. Those who talked most about religion cared least for it; and controversies about doubtful things, and things of little moment, ate up all zeal for things which were practicable and indisputable.

'In countenance,' wrote a friend, 'he appeared to be

of a stern and rough temper, but in his conversation mild and affable; not given to loquacity or to much discourse in company unless some urgent occasion required it; observing never to boast of himself or his parts, but rather to seem low in his own eyes, and submit himself to the judgment of others; abhorring lying and swearing, being just, in all that lay in his power, to his word; not seeming to revenge injuries, loving to reconcile differences and make friendships with all. He had a sharp quick eye, with an excellent discerning of persons, being of good judgment and quick wit.' 'He was tall of stature, strong boned, though not corpulent, somewhat of a ruddy face, with sparkling eyes, wearing his hair on his upper lip; his hair reddish, but in his later days time had sprinkled it with grey; his nose well set, but not declining or bending; his mouth moderate large, his forehead something high, and his habit always plain and modest.'

He was himself indifferent to advancement, and he did not seek it for his family. A London merchant offered to take his son into his house. 'God,' he said, 'did not send me to advance my family, but to preach the Gospel.' He had no vanity—an exemption extremely rare in those who are personally much before the public. The personal popularity was in fact the part of his situation which he least liked. When he was to preach in London, 'if there was but one day's notice the meeting house was crowded to overflowing.' Twelve hundred people would be found collected before seven o'clock on a dark winter's morning to hear a lecture from him. In Zoar Street, Southwark, his church was sometimes so crowded that he had to be lifted to the pulpit stairs over the congregation's heads. It pleased him, but he was on the watch against the pleasure of being himself admired. A friend compli-

mented him once after service, on 'the sweet sermon
which he had delivered. 'You need not remind me of
that,' he said. 'The Devil told me of it before I was out
of the pulpit.'

'Conviction of sin' has become a conventional phrase,
shallow and ineffective even in those who use it most
sincerely. Yet moral evil is still the cause of nine-tenths
of the misery in the world, and it is not easy to measure
the value of a man who could prolong the conscious sense
of the deadly nature of it, even under the forms of a
decomposing theology. Times are changing. The intellectual current is bearing us we know not where, and the
course of the stream is in a direction which leads us
far from the conclusions in which Bunyan and the
Puritans established themselves; but the truths which
are most essential for us to know cannot be discerned
by speculative arguments. Chemistry cannot tell us why
some food is wholesome and other food is poisonous.
That food is best for us which best nourishes the body
into health and strength; and a belief in a Supernatural
Power which has given us a law to live by and to which
we are responsible for our conduct, has alone, of all the
influences known to us, succeeded in ennobling and
elevating the character of man. The particular theories
which men have formed about it have often been wild
and extravagant. Imagination, agitated by fear or
stimulated by pious enthusiasm, has peopled heaven with
demigods and saints—creations of fancy, human forms
projected upon a mist and magnified into celestial images.
How much is true of all that men have believed in past
times and have now ceased to believe, how much has been a
too eager dream, no one now can tell. It may be that other
foundations may be laid hereafter for human conduct on

which an edifice can be raised no less fair and beautiful; but no signs of it are as yet apparent.

So far as we yet know, morality rests upon a sense of obligation; and obligation has no meaning except as implying a Divine command, without which it would cease to be. Until 'duty' can be presented to us in a shape which will compel our recognition of it with equal or superior force, the passing away of 'the conviction of sin' can operate only to obscure our aspirations after a high ideal of life and character. The scientific theory may be correct, and it is possible that we may be standing on the verge of the most momentous intellectual revolution which has been experienced in the history of our race. It may be so, and also it may not be so. It may be that the most important factors in the scientific equation are beyond the reach of human intellect. However it be, the meat which gives strength to the man is poison to the child; and as yet we are still children, and are likely to remain children. 'Every relief from outward restraint,' says one who was not given to superstition, 'if it be not attended with increased power of self-command, is simply fatal.' Men of intelligence, therefore, to whom life is not a theory, but a stern fact, conditioned round with endless possibilities of wrong and suffering, though they may never again adopt the letter of Bunyan's creed, will continue to see in conscience an authority for which culture is no substitute; they will conclude that in one form or other responsibility is not a fiction but a truth; and, so long as this conviction lasts, the 'Pilgrim's Progress' will still be dear to all men of all creeds who share in it, even though it pleases the 'elect' modern philosophers to describe its author as a 'Philistine of genius.'

Spottiswoode & Co., Printers, New-street Square, London.

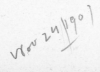

Now publishing, in crown 8vo. price 2s. 6d. each,

ENGLISH MEN OF LETTERS.

Edited by JOHN MORLEY.

JOHNSON. By LESLIE STEPHEN. Crown 8vo. 2s. 6d.

'The new series opens well with Mr. Leslie Stephen's sketch of Dr. Johnson. It could hardly have been done better, and it will convey to the readers for whom it is intended a juster estimate of Johnson than either of the two essays of Lord Macaulay.'—PALL MALL GAZETTE.

SCOTT. By R. H. HUTTON. Crown 8vo. 2s. 6d.

'We could not wish for a more suggestive introduction to Scott and his poems and novels.'—EXAMINER.

GIBBON. By J. C. MORISON. Crown 8vo. 2s. 6d.

'As a clear, thoughtful, and attractive record of the life and works of the greatest among the world's historians, it deserves the highest praise.'
EXAMINER.

SHELLEY. By J. A. SYMONDS. Crown 8vo. 2s. 6d.

'The lovers of this great poet are to be congratulated at having at their command so fresh, clear, and intelligent a presentment of the subject, written by a man of adequate and wide culture.'—ATHENÆUM.

HUME. By Professor HUXLEY, F.R.S. Crown 8vo. 2s. 6d.

'It may fairly be said that no one now living could have expounded Hume with more sympathy or with equal perspicuity.'—ATHENÆUM.

GOLDSMITH. By WILLIAM BLACK. Crown 8vo. 2s. 6d.

'Mr. Black brings a fine sympathy and taste to bear in his criticism of Goldsmith's writings, as well as his sketch of the incidents of his life.'
ATHENÆUM.

DEFOE. By W. MINTO. Crown 8vo. 2s. 6d.

'Mr. Minto's book is careful and accurate in all that is stated, and faithful in all that it suggests. It will repay reading more than once.'
ATHENÆUM.

BURNS. By Principal SHAIRP. Crown 8vo. 2s. 6d.

' It is impossible to desire fairer criticism than Principal Shairp's on Burns's poetry. . . . None of the series has given a truer estimate either of character or of genius than this volume.'—SPECTATOR.

SPENSER. By the Very Rev. the DEAN OF ST. PAUL'S. Crown 8vo. 2s 6d.

' Dr. Church is master of his subject, and writes always with good taste.'—ACADEMY.

THACKERAY. By ANTHONY TROLLOPE. Crown 8vo. 2s. 6d.

' Mr. Trollope's sketch is excellently adapted to fulfil the purpose of the series in which it appears.'—ATHENÆUM.

BURKE. By JOHN MORLEY. Crown 8vo. 2s. 6d.

' It is no disparagement to the literary studies already published in this admirable series, to say that none of them have surpassed, while few have equalled, this volume on Burke.'—BRITISH QUARTERLY REVIEW.

MILTON. By MARK PATTISON. Crown 8vo. 2s. 6d.

' The writer knows the times and the man, and of both he has written with singular force and discrimination.'—SPECTATOR.

HAWTHORNE. By HENRY JAMES. Crown 8vo. 2s. 6d.

SOUTHEY. By Professor DOWDEN. Crown 8vo. 2s. 6d.

BUNYAN. By JAMES A. FROUDE. Crown 8vo. 2s. 6d.

CHAUCER. By Professor A. W. WARD. Crown 8vo. 2s. 6d.

IN PREPARATION.

WORDSWORTH. By F. W. H. MYERS.

SWIFT. By JOHN MORLEY.

BYRON. By Professor NICHOL.

COWPER. By GOLDWIN SMITH. [Shortly.

ADAM SMITH. By LEONARD H. COURTNEY.

BENTLEY. By Professor R. C. JEBB.

LANDOR. By Professor SIDNEY COLVIN.

POPE. By LESLIE STEPHEN. [Shortly.

Others will follow.

MACMILLAN AND CO., LONDON.